Margaret Atwood's

This book is due on the last date stamped below.
Failure to return books on the date due may result
in assessment of overdue fees.

CONTINUUM CONTEMPORARIES

## Also available in this series

## Forthcoming in this series:

· **MARGARET ATWOOD'S**

*Alias Grace*

A READER'S GUIDE

**GINA WISKER**

CONTINUUM | NEW YORK | LONDON

2002

The Continuum International Publishing Group Inc
370 Lexington Avenue, New York, NY 10017

The Continuum International Publishing Group Ltd
The Tower Building, 11 York Road, London SE1 7NX

*www.continuumbooks.com*

Printed in the United States of America

Library of Congress Cataloging-in-Publication Data

Wisker, Gina, 1951–
      Margaret Atwood's Alias Grace : a reader's guide / Gina Wisker.
          p. cm. — (Continuum contemporaries)
      Includes bibliographical references and index.
      ISBN 0-8264-5706-1 (pbk. : alk. paper)
      1. Atwood, Margaret Eleanor, 1939– Alias Grace.   2. Biographical
fiction — History and criticism.   3. Marks, Grace, b. 1826 — In
literature.   4. Women murderers in literature.   5. Trials (Murder) in
literature.   6. Canada — In literature.   I. Title. II. Series.
      PR9199.3.A8 A7939 2002
      813'.54 — dc21
                                                         2002005625

# *Contents*

# 1

# The Novelist

**M**argaret Atwood is arguably Canada's greatest living writer. She is also a significant contemporary woman writer who has made a distinct contribution to women's writing in the twentieth and twenty-first centuries. Primarily a novelist, Atwood also writes poetry and essays, short stories and criticism, and acts as an editor. She was born November 18, 1939, in Ottowa, Ontario, the second of three children. Until she was twelve she spent most of her summers in the wilds of the northern Quebec and Ontario bush with her family and entomologist father. Dividing time between the bush and the town helped develop a sense of dual identity and allegiance which has informed both imagery and ideas in her work. In 1946, her family moved to Toronto, where she attended high school (1952–1957). Between 1957 and 1961 she studied Honors English (with critic Northrop Frye and Jay Macpherson) at Victoria College, the University of Toronto, graduating in 1961.

**EDUCATION, LOCATION, AWARDS, EARLY WRITING**

Poetry and fiction have both won praise and prizes for Atwood, whose first poetry collection, a privately printed, self-published chapbook, *Double Persephone*, won the E.J. Pratt medal (1961). This was followed by a Woodrow Wilson Fellowship enabling her to become a graduate student at Radcliffe College, Harvard University, Massachusetts. In 1962 she gained her MA and began to read for a Ph.D. at Harvard on "The English Metaphysical Romance." Deciding the academic life (or at least research) was not for her, after all, she interrupted her studies to work for a market-research company in Toronto and to teach English at the University of British Columbia, Vancouver (1964–1965). Here she wrote the first draft of *The Edible Woman*, published in 1969. In 1966 she published *The Circle Game*, receiving the Governor General's Award for Poetry. She followed this with *The Animals in that Country* (1968), *The Journals of Susanna Moodie* and *Procedures for Underground* (1970), and *Power Politics* (1971). Atwood established herself as equally important as both poet and novelist. The publication in 1972 of *Surfacing* and *Survival: A Thematic Guide to Canadian Literature* consolidated her significance as novelist and cultural critic. *The Handmaid's Tale* (1985) and *Cat's Eye* (1988) brought Atwood international fame, consistently confirmed and maintained with her novels and poetry.

Margaret Atwood has lived in Canada, the United States, and Europe. Her work has gained her creative writing posts and roles in key associations from Toronto to New York and Australia. She has won numerous prizes including the Los Angeles Times Prize for Fiction (1986), and been several times shortlisted for the Booker Prize, which she won with *Blind Assassin* in 2000. Her work as an editor is recognized as having been a major influence on bringing

Canadian literature to an international audience and establishing its specific characteristics and relationships with other bodies of work. In 1982 she edited *The New Oxford Book of Canadian Verse in English,* (but she was criticized for including too many women) and in 1986 *The Oxford Book of Canadian Short Stories in English.* Atwood also edited *The CanLit Foodbook* (an alternative cookbook, 1987) and published her own critical writings in *Second Words: Selected Critical Prose* (1982). She is politically and socially involved through PEN and Amnesty International and continues to be active against social injustice.

Atwood's work is read throughout the world and both *Surfacing* and *The Handmaid's Tale* have been made into films. Her writing has had a significant influence on contemporary writing by women, and has brought the re-writing of genre fiction to the fore as a form of cultural critique for postmodernist and other contemporary writing. Many of her works rewrite romantic fictions, and *The Handmaid's Tale* uses science fiction and utopian fiction forms. She articulates and problematizes experiences of women and girls in powerfully moving ways. Her language is beautiful, perceptibly chosen, highlighting ways in which power controls language and shapes people's lives. She depicts history as a partial, often subjectively and politically, shaped construction, and exposes gendered roles as social and cultural constructions, utilizing different forms of expression, different discourses. Atwood exposes constraints, suggesting that behaviors, roles, representations, and versions *could* be different.

## ATWOOD AS A CANADIAN WRITER

Atwood's work began to receive international critical attention in 1972, with the publication of *Surfacing* and her influential critical analysis of Canada's literary tradition, *Survival: A Thematic Guide to Canadian Literature.* Both books consider similar themes, in particular the notion of a victim complex, which Atwood identified as both a woman's and a postcolonial response: "not only the Canadian stance towards the world, but the usual female one." Most Canadian reviewers considered *Surfacing* concerned with nationalism, while Americans treated the book as feminist or ecological (partly, perhaps, because it indicts America as capitalist and imperialist). *Surfacing* concentrates on an exploration of Canadian nationality in relation to the invasive materialism of America. More explicitly, it concentrates on a woman's search for her own identity, in a period when getting in touch with Nature and the self through sloughing off those materialistic constructions was just beginning to dawn, for women at least.

These are continuing issues for her: women's roles, their lives, the ways in which stories are told of, myths constructed about, fictions perpetuated about and by women. While the range of her writing shifts from the wilderness tale, to the comic, the science fictional, the social realist, and the mythic/magical, she continually explores different representations and constructions, emphasizing their fictionality. Atwood also considers ways in which women might use or move beyond these and construct versions of themselves. Her work is a dialogue between popular fictional forms and "high art," that is, the more literary, post-modern work which uses other works intertextually, rewrites and reinterprets history, showing us the everyday and the textual constructedness of versions of our lives.

Margaret Atwood is engaged with issues and lives of others living in Canada. Canadian literature, or "Can lit," as an established identified location for study has only really emerged since 1980. Canadian culture, a "settler-invader" culture, like the Australian with which it is often compared, is somewhat culturally schizophrenic, split between French and English influences in language and history, closely affected by the United States, its near neighbor. This influence is often seen as constant, potential, overshadowing power and vulgarity (W.H. New, 1989) dominating Canada's attempts to establish a clearly distinct identity. From an imperial and colonial point of view, Canada attracted international settlers including Irish, Scottish, and latterly, Japanese. In *Alias Grace*, Grace Marks herself is of Irish immigrant stock. Canada imported English institutions, cultural values, and writing traditions, adding Caribbean influences. In relation to other imperial and now postcolonial nations "Canada . . . has tended to see herself as the undervalued orphan in the imperial family" (Brydon and Tiffin, 1993, p. 63), a "Cinderella" country awaiting her moment. Canada was seeking a national identity while also suffering national disputes, beginning with the Free Trade Agreement with the United States, and problems generated by the failure of the Meech Lake and Charlottetown Accords. One of the intentions of those establishing a sense of the nation and identity of Canada was to construct a shared community rather than an oppositional identity. Canada still sees itself as a culturally harmonious, peaceable kingdom, although much of this is cultural myth.

Although Margaret Atwood rarely talks about indigenous peoples and Japanese settlers, she does deal with the tensions of living as a near neighbor of the more abrasive America. First Nations writers represent Canada and their own lives, the loss of lands and identity, marginalization, and reassertion of cultural difference within a nationally harmonious, homogenizing Canadian culture. More recent settlers deal with the racism, appropriation, and settlement, their lived experience in Canada. An increasingly sensitive issue for settler-originated writers in many different countries, including Canada, has been the concern with finding an appropriate language in which to write. Canadian writers often feel they use "alien" words in a "colonial space" (Brydon, 1981):

It was a situation in which the perceived "inauthenticity" of the spoken New World/Word became the site of investigation and expression—not as the preliminary to a possible "adaptation," but as a continuing dynamic of the use of "alien" words in "colonial space." (Ashcroft, Griffith and Tiffin, 1989, p. 140)

One task for the Canadian writer is to un-write expressions adopted from imperial British, French and American influences.

At one time I considered it to be the task of the Canadian writer to give names to his experience, to be the namer. I now suspect that, on the contrary, it is his task to un-name . . . there is in the Canadian word a concealed other experience, sometimes British, sometimes American. (Kroetsch 1974, p. 43)

Finding appropriate language is a crucial step to enabling a national identity, as Margaret Atwood's own work on Canadian writing and cultural identity testifies. It is an issue concerning Canada's indigenous writers as well as those of British or French descent who often fail to find their experiences represented in the forms and expressions of English or U.S. literature. Atwood found little real Canadian writing prior to the 1970s, and until the 1980s, Canada almost entirely ignored its indigenous (First Nations) people's writing. Women, Atwood argues, are no mere footnotes in the pioneering environment:

Canadians never developed the concept of women as mere brainless decoration. Canadian folklore is still full of tales of our grandmothers' generation when women ran farms, chased off bears, delivered their own babies in remote locations and bit off the umbilical cords. Whatever the reason, if you're looking at writing in Canada, you can't just footnote the women. (Pepinster, 1996, p. 9)

This echoes the kind of "battler" motif found in writing by Carol Shields and Australian settler writers' tales of "the drover's wife." Reading earlier writing helps establish a sense of history for national literatures, but it can also often reinforce myths and stereotypes, a common problem in settler cultures. Pioneers are recognizable figures:

> He stood, a point
> on a sheet of green paper
> proclaiming himself the centre
>
> . . . . .
>
> For many years
> he fished for a great vision,
> dangling the hooks of sown
> roots under the surface
> of the shallow earth.
>
> It was like
> enticing whales with a bent
> pin
> (Atwood, "Progressive Insani-
> ties of a Pioneer" in Thieme,
> 1996, p. 356–7)

Our stories are likely to be tales not of those who made it but of those who made it back, from the awful experience — the North, the snow-storm, the sinking ship — that killed everyone else. The survivor has no triumph or victory but the fact of his survival; he has little after his ordeal that he did not have before, except gratitude for having escaped with his life . . . A preoccupation with one's survival is necessarily also a preoccupation with the obstacles to that survival. (Atwood, 1996, in Thieme, [1972], p. 360)

Atwood rewrites and uses cultural and traditional myths to explore and critique representations and histories of women, of pioneers, and the people (mainly) of Toronto. Her poetry and criticism partner her fictions. One popular myth, overwhelming more radical representations of women in Canadian literature, has traditionally been that of the hardy, pioneering settler woman living a tough life in great hardship — determined to raise her children, provide food, living life in the Canadian bush with grit and zeal, walking through the snow to help sick neighbors, ploughing, suffering from cold and isolation. Some origins of the figure are real, some derive from the fictionalized autobiography of Susanna Moodie, *Roughing it in the Bush or Life in Canada* (1988 [1852]). Moodie's and settler women's were harsh lives which fascinated Margaret Atwood, who determined to both rewrite and reimagine them. In 1970, rewriting Susannah Moodie in a poetry sequence as *The Journals of Susannah Moodie* (1970), she challenges the stereotype of the tough settler woman, producing a modern work of consciousness rather than a realistic diary, highlighting themes popularized by Moodie and her followers. Atwood brought Moodie to life for twentieth-century readers, twentieth-century women's consciousness registering the paradox of her situation. Moodie visited Grace Marks in the penitentiary, representing her in a way Atwood first took as the whole truth, later discovering it to be subjective.

In 1972 *Survival* followed, beginning to define the character of Canadian literature in relation to, and apart from, that of the United States and UK. In the same year Atwood's novel *Surfacing* (1972)was published, a powerful tale using the survival theme, investigating and challenging stereotypes of Canadian womanhood, positioning the U.S. ways as destructive, hypocritical, and superficial. The protagonist returns to an island in the Canadian wilderness where she lived as a child, to search for her father, a lone forest dweller and student of American Indian lore, missing for nearly a month. With her she takes three companions, one woman and two men, Canadian nationalists who loathe the intrusion of the American versions of Canada and wilderness but have themselves lost all contact with the natural wild land. The novel has been seen as a search for Canadian identity, for religious and spiritual vision, testimony to her relationship with nature. The unnamed heroine rejects American men, offspring of popular culture and precursors of tourists seeking a "modified wilderness experience":

It wasn't the men I hated, it was the Americans, the human beings, men and women both. They'd had their chance but they had turned against the gods and it was time for me to choose sides. (Atwood, 1972, p. 154)

In Atwood's writing here, "American" denotes a homogenizing imperialism that cannot tolerate difference, "a tendency that can characterise American feminism as well as American imperialism" (Brydon and Tiffin, 1993, p. 94). She positions herself away from the Americans' technologically adept invasiveness, and toward the native gods of the place. By doing so she aligns herself with the "myth of Canadian identity as an alternative way of being North American" (Brydon and Tiffin, 1993, p. 94). The issue of hunting animals just for the kill is important in this novel. Canadians can be hunters but, Atwood argues, not in the name of overindulgence or fun, seen as superficiality inherent in the American way. Central to this argument in the novel is the image of the heron, beautiful in flight, later crumpled and dead.

The novel is a quest for identity. In denying her name "I no longer have a name. I tried for all these years to be civilised but I'm not and I'm through pretending" (p. 168), the protagonist also rejects the need to name wild creatures and places, a link between naming, language and civilization's limitations. *Surfacing* is an example of second wave feminism, recuperating myths of women's identities which have constrained and misrepresented women as

guilty for the world's ills (Pandora, Eve) sexually dangerous, predatory, and destructive (Medusa, mermaids). The protagonist under-
goes various stages of quests similar to those of mythic females. Like
Persephone, she descends into a world of the dead, plunging into a
glacial lake, the site of her childhood. There she discovers her
father's body. She returns to the wilderness, a natural state, sleeps
fitfully, prowling on all fours, feeding off roots and berries. The
heroine's personal crisis causes a breakdown which is also a break-
through, a familiar 1970s theme in women's writing. She decides to
atone for an earlier abortion, a sacrifice to technology and male
invasion, and to conceive and bear a child in a totally natural earth-
linked and located manner, just as the child of *herself* starts to
resurface.

This time I will do it by myself, squatting, on old newspapers in a corner
alone; or on leaves, dry leaves, a heap of them, that's cleaner. The baby
will slip out easily as an egg, a kitten, and I'll lick it off and bite the cord,
the blood returning to the ground where it belongs, the moon will be full,
pulling. In the morning I would be able to see it: it will be covered with
shining fur, a god, I will never teach it any words. (p. 162)

She feels totally at one with the natural world, blurring her identity
with that of trees, a frog, anything natural: "I lean against a tree, I
am a tree leaning. . . . I am not an animal or a tree, I am the thing,
in which the trees and animals move and grow" (p. 181). Exiting
her trance state, she views with interest her matted hair and wild
appearance, deciding to take this new found sense of self as survivor,
no victim, and live differently back in the civilized city world. It is
a powerful, sensitive, rather "green" novel, visionary, feminist,
aligned to reclaimed, rewritten myths and versions of woman as
earth mother, at one with nature, and it helped to establish Atwood
as both a woman writer and a Canadian writer.

## OTHER KEY NOVELS

Other novels by Atwood use humor and irony to critique Canadian ways of life and women's representation and stereotyping. *The Edible Woman* (1969) indicts relationships which figuratively devour women, focusing on Marion who works in sales and marketing (as did Atwood). About to marry Peter, Marion realizes her role is so dependent upon his version of her that she equates his engulfing and devouring of her personality with a form of cannibalism. Once she has identified herself with food, she becomes acutely aware of the disgusting nature of people eating, enhanced by her pregnant friend Ainsley's delight in eating for two and self-identification with food and baby production. Like Katherine Mansfield's *In a German Pension* stories, the equation between birth, marriage, engulfment/ engulfing and digesting food is made revoltingly clear. Marion can eat nothing. Her cathartic moment comes when she manages to shake off the oppressive relationship with Peter, offering him a grotesque, cake version of herself. Having exterminated her sense of imminent consumption as part of someone else's self-enhancing staple diet, Marion returns to normality and eating. The book is funny and topical, equating issues of eating with identity, and critiquing the oppressive containment of stereotypical relationships. *Lady Oracle* (1976), also amusing, rewrites romantic fiction while dealing, as does *Alias Grace*, with the fascination of New Age religion, spiritualism, and seances. *Bodily Harm* (1981) directly equates the food metaphor with an oppressive sexual relationship. Laura, in trading her body, resembles a consumable.

## *The Handmaid's Tale*

*The Handmaid's Tale* (1985) was Atwood's first best-selling novel. Containing a dedication to her ancestor who was hanged as a witch (but survived — presumably proving she *was* a witch), *The Handmaid's Tale* differs greatly from her previous work, more obviously set in contemporary Canada. It depicts the antifeminist distopia of Gilead, using science fiction formulae to critique ways in which social politics and reproductive technologies constrain women. This concern was highly topical among second wave feminists and the "take back the night" marches of the novel were also topical, so it acts as both a comment on its own times and a project forward of characteristics of those times into a distopian future. In a post-holocaust future, women are kept in different roles, defined by their labor, of which breeding is seen as a key element. This feminist, highly political novel exposes the psychological, cultural, and legal structures and constraints which repress people and enforce often unjust, absurd laws, rules, and roles.

The taped story of narrator Offred is discovered in an archive by future historians. Religiously garbed "handmaid" because of her potential to bear children in a post-holocaust, infertile world of tyrannically enforced patriarchy, Offred's enforced subservience to the body, procreation, and a subordinate role within a household containing a military male, a non-procreative, cosmetic companion Wife, and drudges or "Marthas," is a terrifying potential future for women. Language is coded, thoughts seem policed, and all sexual freedoms have been lost. While past films illustrate the vulnerability and inequalities of women in the latter part of the twentieth century, these freedoms are preferable over the tyranny and lies of the future state. It is a terrifying, polemically powerful, feminist sci-fi novel.

Both realistic and fantastic, Atwood's works take cultural myths and investigate their roots, overturn, expose and undercut them, mixing details of everyday life with equally rich details of myth and metaphor.

## *The Robber Bride*

*The Robber Bride* (1993) is a Gothic marriage tale highlighting the pleasures and dangers of male/ female relationships and sisterhood. The story itself derives from a fairy tale "The Robber Bridegroom" in which a male robber, a kind of peasant Bluebeard, tricks a series of hapless brides into marriage. His mother colludes, the girls turn into victims — he hacks them to pieces and devours them. In Atwood's version, the robber bridegroom is replaced with a powerful, intrusive female robber bride, Zenia, really a Gothic product of the fears and desires of the other women in the novel. Zenia consistently manages to infiltrate the relationships of those around her by investigating and persuading others to trust and confide in her, turning their weaknesses against them. In each case she steals their male partners for herself. This intrusion and resulting theft is always based on the weakness of the relationship, its basis in fantasy and deception. Zenia, a product of their imaginations but very palpably real, emerges from each woman at a certain stage in their development.

Charis, Toni, and Roz, three friends like the mythical three graces, each hold a version of life and a weakness. Each represents roles women can take. Identity is a theme. The characters' identities are formed from each other, and from the opportunities of the times in which they live, the myths and socially constructed versions of what women can be in this society. They are also produced and constructed, marked off against the "Other", the predatory Zenia. Zenia herself is a construction grown from their own fears, the tales they tell her of what terrified them in their past — destroying mothers (Charis), parental suicide (Toni), attempts to please, losses. These fears are scenarios Zenia proceeds to realize. Arriving on a wind like the wicked witch in the Wizard of Oz, Zenia is vampiric, both a projection of, and feeder from, others' fears. Like a vampire she has to be invited in, transforming herself into the shape and problems these women wish to nurture, help, and relate to, undermining them, embodying their weak spots.

A macabre Gothic fantasy, the novel investigates versions of sexuality, gender roles, male/ female relationships and female/ female relationships. Like *Alias Grace*, it is meta-fictional, playing with and commenting on the power of language, of memory and history. History, neither fixed nor dependable, is clearly a construction. Military historian Tony constructs and re-writes, replays history regularly in her own job, and Zenia retells her own history, skilled in dramatic representations of self, of disguises, producing lurid versions: a Russian, a refugee, a child prostitute. As in Tony's lectures, versions unravel and history, seen as a construct, pinned down by military tactics, nonetheless evades real comprehension.

Identity is questioned, and so too is the order of the narrative. Versions of time, reality, history, and self are shown as constructs, memory as undependable: "memory divides, into what she wanted to happen and what actually did happen" (p. 153).

Margaret Atwood has designed the covers of some of her own poetry collections and, in the seventies, she published a cartoon strip satirizing Canadian nationalism and sexual politics, favorite subjects of her early work. Visual art figures in *Cat's Eye* (1988), reinforcing arguments concerning the inability of myths and systems to impose order on and interpret reality. Her novels might be balanced and structured, but her characters exemplify and dramatize the impossibility of imposing order on reality, defining fixed identity, and representing true historical facts. *Lady Oracle* provides a romantic parody (1976) of romantic fictional interpretations of reality while the post-modern, rewritten fairytale *The Robber Bride* (1993) shows secret desires to find refuge in systems, patterns, and accepted visions and versions of self and of history ultimately shown as absurd and pointless. Self is multiple, as is the record of events, personal history, and public history. All Atwood's novels use the characteristics of and subvert traditional genres, showing how their formulae reinforce or expose society's constraints.

## The Blind Assassin

Her first novel of the twenty first century, *The Blind Assassin* won the Booker prize and, like *Alias Grace*, sets different narratives side by side. It mixes the fictional with semi-fictionalized autobiographical forms, interspersing these versions of what is or what *happened*, what people might be like, with constructions from journalism and other public documentations. With both novels it is clear that we and our society are all in the fictionalizing business. Records, representations, and interpretations are constructions of the real, whether concretely experienced or the real of the imagination.

*The Blind Assassin* is a layered text exploring the lives of two sisters. Its complex form resembles a Chinese puzzle, a novel within a novel within a novel. A family memoir by Iris Chase, daughter of a wealthy Canadian button manufacturer ruined in the Depression, the frame tale focuses on the death of Laura Chase, Iris's sister who drove her car off a bridge after the war, taking it into the famous Toronto gorge, beloved of suicides. Laura (it seems) wrote one rather shocking and daring romantic fiction novel which made her name, before dying young. Laura's life and her love of the political Alex Thompson is part of Iris's narrative. As an octogenarian, Iris recalls their childhood, the romantic story they were told about the meeting and love of their parents and their mother's work in the war, followed by their hard drinking, physically and emotionally war damaged father's return and their mother's death. There are many missing or dead mothers in Atwood, like so many other contemporary women writers' work. The father consigns them to a series of ineffectual governesses and tutors. One is a pedophile and bully. Another, of whom they are quite fond, is a dreamer. No one can really control the girls. They develop apart from the working class children in their father's factory, aware of the need to wear the right clothes and yet wishing to be beyond the boundaries of social niceties, askance in their view of constructed versions of behavior and life. Surrounded by people, especially the housekeeper Renie, who deals in clichés and idiomatic expressions, Iris grows up a conformist to maintain family economic stability, while Laura is more vulnerable, troubled by taking everything literally, believing herself the cause of their mother's death.

The narrator's recall brings history to light in a personalized way, emphasizing, as in *Alias Grace*, how we all interpret and select versions of our own memories, fictionalizing our pasts to form a sense of identity. Within the frame of Iris's doctored memoir is the second box of the narrative version of events—clearly fictional, a steamy romance, but bearing a great deal of resemblance to the outward incidences and details of the love affair Iris herself has. This tale, ostensibly *Laura's* fiction, her novel published to scandal and some acclaim, is actually by Iris. Versions of the constructedness of life appear in this romantic fictional narrative. The story of two lovers parallels those of Iris and Alex. The tale is one of love, sexual involvement, class difference, politics, and wild imagination. A third boxed narrative contains the science fiction tales the male protagonist tells his female lover in their snatched moments together under trees and in borrowed rooms. Here they construct a world which, in its sci-fi format, rather bizarrely echoes extremes of their everyday world, but also demonstrates a criticism of the oppressive representations of women in myth and culture. It provides insights into the male narrator's versions of life and women. He peoples his tale with muted beautiful women, sacrificed in lieu of the daughters of the upper classes, and blind assassins, working class heroes of sorts driven by the agendas of politicians to murder the girls, victims to a mythical set of beliefs related to the continuance of society. No one really believes in the myths anymore but they seem to need to perpetuate their paraphernalia. Girls continue to die, assassins to murder, and kings to rule rather pointlessly and vacuously. Like society people, things go on, myths continue their basis in reality rather removed and surreal.

*The Blind Assassin* evidences and explores very different fictional narratives which represent versions and shapes of lives. We are unsure of whether Laura drove away from the ridge deliberately or accidentally became stuck in a railtrack. The public reading, even the court reading, is of misadventure. We are never certain how to fix and represent the truth, always filtered through the narrator, always a construction and interpretation. Atwood's text problematizes documentary evidence, journalist reports, and media write-ups, first person narratives from Iris, as well as fictional narratives in popular fictional forms. Crime narratives occur in the various accidental deaths and misadventure befalling this family, romantic fictions in Laura's/Iris's own novel, science fiction in the narrative within her novel. Other fictional misrepresentations appear in clichéd idiomatic expressions with which Renie constructs and interprets events — taken literally by Laura. We can never grasp whatever the real might be.

Like Grace Marks, Laura and Iris seem part of Toronto history, although the exact truth of this history is even less certain that that of Grace Marks' life. It is a fascinating tale of arson and deaths. Who can we trust? This novel comes closer to *Alias Grace* the more we focus on it. Dealing with social identity, deception, false memory, and deliberately collusive fallible narrative, it casts a very dubious light on the certainty of any kind of record, highlighting constructedness and fictionalization. Like *Alias Grace*, it casts similar light on journalism and historical record, showing them to be partial constructs springing from the concerns of particular periods. Narrative voices are biased and fallible. The tale is, like *Alias Grace*, something of a "Murder mystery" in that it relies upon our seeking after certain truths, hides details, whisks victims away, and pretends to offer clues leading to resolution while forging the links.

Fables parallel real events and Atwood is as concerned with writing a version of Toronto as she is producing sci-fi and other narrative forms. It is in this novel more than anywhere else, that Atwood shows herself to be an urban cartographer of Toronto, both its geography of ravines and bridges, and its psychology. The novel pulls together myths and folktales of materialistic 1970s Toronto and recognizable people and events, used as material for fiction and so:

> *In restaurants we argue*
> *over who will pay for your funeral*
> *though the real question is*
> *whether or not I shall make you immortal*
> *(1970s poem)*

The immortality is a result of the fictionalizing.

Identity, domestic relationships, discovery of the self, critique of the constraints on women's roles and opportunities, fictionalizing, and a Canadian quality dominate all Atwood's novels.

# 2

# The Novel

Perhaps I will tell you lies (p. 41).

I knew I'd remembered it wrong, and the real song said the pig was eat and Tom was beat, and then went howling down the street; but I didn't see why I should make it come out in a better way; and as long as I told no-one of what was on my mind, there was no-one to hold me to account, or correct me, just as there was no-one to say that the real sunrise was nothing like the line I'd invented for myself, but was instead only a soiled yellowish white, like a dead fish in the harbour.

At least in the Lunatic asylum you could see out better. (p. 238)

## STORY/STORIES

It is not a murder mystery, it is a mystery about murder. . . . In a murder mystery you have to come up with the solution, or the readers will rise up against you. You can't just end it by saying, "Well, I don't know."(Atwood interview in Basbanes, 2001)

The story of Grace Marks, possible murderess, possible innocent, is one which captivated the imaginations of late nineteenth century Toronto, as it did of Margaret Atwood and of her readership. Part of its fascination emanates from its basis in the truth, and the sheer impossibility of tracking down that truth, dependent as we all are on historical records, and here on fictionalized, often possibly elaborately ambiguous accounts.

Margaret Atwood retells the real story of Grace Marks and her life in the afterward of the novel. In Ontario in 1843, Grace Marks, a servant girl aged 16, was found guilty of the murders of Thomas Kinnear, her employer, and Nancy Montgomery, his housekeeper. Grace's accomplice, James McDermott, was hanged and she was given a life sentence. She spent thirty years in Kingston penitentiary. After petitions in her favor supporting her innocence or her redemption, in 1872 she was finally granted a pardon and freed.

Grace Marks' story is one well documented in various histories of the 1840s, found in both the journalistic and commentary records such as prison registers and in the diary accounts of Susanna Moodie. Grace, an Irish immigrant of a poor, large, and neglected family, suffered childhood and adolescent abuse. She met up with Nancy Montgomery and was invited to take a job in Mr. Kinnear's household where she seemed to establish a romantic relationship with James McDermott, a stable hand who also worked there. Grace came to public notice when she and James conspired to murder both Mr. Kinnear and Nancy Montgomery the housekeeper, his lover, who was pregnant with his child. They escaped and went on the run. Grace's friend Mary Whitney was, she claimed, actually responsible for the murders. This has been represented as a case of duplicitous transference — Grace blaming her dead friend, claiming that Mary did carry out the murder or that she was Mary when she did it. This psychological defense was complex enough to cast some doubt on her own sanity or at least her deliberate culpability.

While James was hanged, Grace was imprisoned, but her careful behavior in prison led to the Governor's wife's social adoption of her. While Grace did various tasks in the warden's wife's house she was also presented as a fascinating case, attracting local notice among those who wished to rehabilitate others, and who were fascinated with Grace's tale of possession and her potential innocence. The scrapbooks the warden's wife kept of criminals became added to by Grace's presence as a real criminal. Local and national groups and individuals grouped together to attempt to save her or clear her name. One element of this mission came to the knowledge of and then involved the calling in of a young psychologist, Dr. Simon Jordan who planned to work closely with and observe Grace. Jordan is Atwood's invention. The aim was to discover whether she was guilty, but also what caused her actions and her version of them, to understand her psychologically in order to psychoanalyze her (before the term appeared with the work of Jung and Freud). Simon Jordan became spellbound by Grace, in fact he seemed to fall in love with her or be fascinated enough as if in love. The fascination depended on her gradually telling him her tale, or so it seems, although she kept more of it back than she revealed, and he could never determine what was true or false. Grace's tale also drew the interest of a traveling player and magician Jeremiah, a charlatan, the wandering peddler who used to visit the Kinnear household prior to disappearing and reemerging in rather grander clothes and role. Jeremiah the peddler could well have had something to do with the murders, but this is never revealed.

### PERSONAL AND PUBLIC

The story unfolds itself through a series of public community and personal records, letters, ballad, journalism, and contemporary accounts including Susanna Moodie's. Grace's perspective is a first person account, which adds to its credibility, while a third person account emerges from Simon Jordan the young psychoanalyst, whose plans, thoughts, experiences, and interpretations of what he hears from Grace are told using free indirect speech. This form rather puts Simon under scrutiny similar to that of Grace, and indeed, Simon's rather sexually fraught confused memories and dreams place him and Grace almost equally in our minds and imaginations. His fascination with her story mimics our own, her styling it to fit his emerging inclinations, his versions, renders increasingly doubtful the veracity of the tale as it is presented.

"I was to have a happy ending" (p. 446) says Grace, released in 1872, suggesting the fictional even as she records her last day in the prison, and her bizarre insistence on keeping a prison nightdress as keepsake. Grace, her story told, is released to marry a childhood friend, Jamie Walsh, giving both of them the opportunity for happiness. However, he testified against her—a rather troubling scenario. The fiction(alizing) does not stop here. Grace's own record of the time after release relates incidents in her life, imprisonment, and release, as if a story in a book, so continuing to support our sense of its constructedness, its undependability.

We never discover the absolute truth of whether Grace did or did not commit the murder for which she was convicted, or exactly what her role was on the day. No version of the tale ever directly records the events—they are always translated and transmuted, avoiding the full details. The novel resembles a patchwork quilt. The variety of tales—ballad, first person narrative, confession, and so on which constitute the record of events need interpreting in relation to their genre and context. Reading Grace's story in the context of the variety of other records, the third person narration, interspersing Simon Jordan's dreams and visions and various letters, refuses the imposition of a single version and pattern.

## REALISM AND FORMS OF FICTIONALIZING

The actual case on which this novel is based is famous in terms of how it is represented but a little vaguer as a recording of truth and hard fact. On July 23, 1843, the wealthy Ontario farmer Thomas Kinnear and his young housekeeper, Nancy Montgomery, were murdered. James McDermott, Kinnear's recently employed stable hand and the 16-year-old Irish immigrant Grace, the servant girl, were convicted, McDermott of the murder, Grace as his accomplice. McDermott was hanged, while Grace Marks' sentence was commuted to life, and on November 19, 1843 she entered the Kingston, Ontario Provincial penitentiary.

*Alias Grace* takes place in several time frames, but two in particular. One is in the present of 1851 as Grace works in the prison Governor's house and is psychoanalyzed by Simon Jordan. This episode moves into a later time, when her case is taken up further by local well-wishers and she works with a spiritualist charlatan, Jeremiah the ex-peddler. These events end in 1872, when Grace is released and marries. The present and current tale is interspersed with tales or recollections of her past, mainly focusing on eight years previously (1843) when the murders were committed, but also revealing some more distant past events in Grace's childhood. The account relies upon a series of openly verbalized or hidden first person narratives which record and recall the past, providing versions of the key event eight years previously: the murders of

Mr. Kinnear, Grace's employer, and Nancy the housekeeper. It is these murders which form the focal point of the narrative causing us to ask (and Grace to refuse to answer) whether she did or did not commit the murders with (if he was) her lover, James McDermott.

This seemingly straightforward question is increasingly difficult to answer the more Grace provides or reconfigures versions of her story. She keeps a great deal from us, and a great deal from herself. It is impossible to finally judge the extent of her collusion, so embroiled is she in other forms of cultural collusion, which would assume her innocence or accidental naïve involvement. The further historical layer is uncovered of Grace's youth as an Irish immigrant and settler in Canada, and of events leading to the murders. There are letters, and a third person narrative in the present tense that makes the tale immediate, seemingly dependable, like a witness account of a crime. It is of course both a crime tale, depending on and charted through public records, and a first person testimony, the uneasy relationship between these being exactly the right gap down which the reader falls attempting to "fix" a true history. Grace is our unreliable witness, our main fallible narrator.

Grace tells her story to Simon Jordan the young doctor, but she also tells it to us through her first person narrative which seems to be less a set of thoughts and a straightforward factual memory than a form like an inner diary, an (actually) unspoken journal. Neither form can be trusted, as the epigraph quotations above suggest. She even embellishes the truth consciously to herself and oscillates between a prosaic and a lyrical record as if deliberately positioning herself as either or, both, speaker or reader. In true post-modernist form, the variety of accounts enables us to question the nature of all records wherever they appear on the continuum of seemingly factual or overtly fictional representations and records of events.

Grace, a housemaid and possible (probable?) murderer of house-keeper Nancy and house owner Mr. Kinnear, tells her own tale of the events which cause the police to capture her and her lover, put him to death, and place her in an asylum. There is a medley of other records from the actual period in which the murders took place and in which Grace was imprisoned: witness reports, (one from Susanna Moodie) journalist and medical reports, legal records, and an image or two. They pull together a complex, contradictory picture, providing alternative readings of events to those given us by Grace and preventing readers from discovering which are fabricated.

Grace's thoughts turn on recall of the events of the past, comments about the treatment she receives, and more general comments about roles which women are expected to play. The Governor's wife's visitors and popular opinion indicate that women are morally spineless, weak, ornamental, undependable, somewhat gullible and naïve, and easily led astray. It is this kind of assumption about women which lies behind the executing of McDermott, the man in the murder, and the incarceration of Grace, the woman. Such a gender-based discriminatory practice could possibly be seen as either kindly or founded upon some investment in Grace's actual innocence. In fact, it was more likely to be based on a certain incredulity that a woman could commit such a brutal act, and on a belief that naturally gentle, naïve, gullible creatures (women) were likely to have so behaved only if led astray. Grace could be such a case, or she could be aware of such constructions of women, and, equally aware of the performative nature of women's roles in society, could be playing to the well-intentioned, naïve, gender-biased views of those around her. As such, then, the novel is partly about ways in which women are misrepresented, and partly about ways in which all methods of recording and retelling history and experience are themselves flawed and fictive. The novel deals with identity and truth, testimony and history, fictions and records, and it asks: Which alias is real? Where is Grace?

## FORMS AND STYLE

The events leading up to the murders are revealed through narrative, letters, newspaper accounts, excerpts from the recorder of life in the Canada bush, Susanna Moodie's journal, notes by doctors and wardens, and poems by Robert Browning, Emily Dickinson, and Alfred Lord Tennyson. These latter contextualize it as a tale of women's incarceration and deception, lingering and loss, a Victorian romance of a certain kind of subjection, the sacrifice of woman to a Victorian Ideal, and, through literary references, a certain kind of mythologizing and fictionalizing about women's lives and roles.

Symbols and leitmotifs are significant. Grace is aware that as a woman she is bound to be designated both the author of any original sin and possibly also too delicate to have committed any sin. She deals with images and references to apples, the Garden of Eden, and fruit in art. Bringing her various fruits and vegetables is one way Simon Jordan seems to invite her to retell her story and revive her memories. Christopher Lehmann-Haupt (online 2001) comments:

the apple Simon offers Grace initiates an intricate symbolic working out of the Eden myth that ultimately resolves itself in Grace's theory that only one tree existed in Paradise, and that the Fruit of Life and the Fruit of Good and Evil were the same.

The novel is divided into chapters which each take their names from quilt patterns. Grace Marks, as a servant, would have found much of her everyday pleasure in quilt-making and acknowledges this as she works and sews in the Governor's house. Quilting and stitchwork are not only traditional female activities, they are also seen historically as therapeutic. In the early nineteenth century, in her work to improve the lot of female prisoners in Newgate, Elizabeth Fry introduced needlework and knitting to develop habits and rewards of industry.

The different types of quilt pattern structure and parallel the process of reading the novel. We try to piece together into some overall pattern or shape versions of Grace's story and various public interpretations of it: ballad, journalism, prison record, Susannah Moodie's tale, Grace's own narrative recollections or constructions for herself and Simon Jordan, and so on. As a highly domestic activity, quilting aligns Grace with other artistic women whose work was confined to the domestic sphere. Grace's construction work resembles that of women writers, suggesting artifice. Her quilt is a creative product, so too is her story. Quilting connotes sisterhood and speaking out, coded patterns, the opposite of clear messages. African American Alice Walker uses quilting in *The Color Purple* to indicate ways in which women expressed both their creativity and their sisterly solidarity. Atwood uses patchwork as a medium through which we can construct and read Grace, expert quiltmaker. It also acts as a metaphor for the literary artefact, the novel itself.

Quiltmaking, as a form of female discourse, empowers Grace to speak in a language not universally accessible. It enables her to express some of her hidden thoughts and sub or unconscious recollections and to withold secrets from Simon Jordan, her male inquisitor, who uses the traditional method of suggestion by association to plumb the depths of Grace's memory.

Grace presents for Jordan an idyllic image, sewing in companionable peace with Nancy, James McDermott, her co-accused, and Jamie Walsh, whom she eventually marries :

There we were, in a kind of harmony; and the evening was so beautiful, that it made a pain in my heart . . . and I thought that if I could have a wish, it would be that nothing would ever change, and we could stay that way forever. (p. 230)

The art and form of sewing itself relates to the ways in which retelling an event reshapes it—reminding us that all forms of story-telling and memory are unreliable. Susanna Moodie's tale is no more or less reliable than Atwood's and Grace's own:

". . . Mrs Moodie is a literary lady, and like all such, and indeed like the sex in general, she is inclined to—"
    "Embroider," says Simon. (p. 191)

Another type of patchwork, or album, scrapbook collections are mentioned early in the account of Grace's dealings with Simon accentuating the idea of the novel as an album quilt (Rogerson, p. 199). The Governor's wife and his daughters collect a range of evidence and mementos. The wife collects newspaper cuttings about notorious criminals to "horrify her acquaintances" (p. 26). The more sentimental Lydia collects items, snippets from dresses and clothing from both criminals and friends (preferably dead), and written expressions of undying love from female friends : "little scraps of cloth from their dresses, little snippets of ribbon, pictures cut from magazines" (p. 25). In Lydia's collection, a scarf reminds her of a drowned friend. Grace's own contributions to the "album quilt" of the novel focus on similar themes: crime, friendship, love, and death.

Quilting block patterns provide a graphic structure to the novel, and also hint at some of the themes explored in chapters and sections which they introduce. They take several literary forms. The second block, "Rocky Road," is a poem. The fourth, "A Young

Man's Fancy," consists of a number of letters and a third-person narrative involving Simon and a monologue from Grace. The variety within and between the sections reflects the quilt metaphor, suggesting differences in color and texture and differences between the patterns of the individual blocks.

Grace fabricates her various versions of her tale, and we try putting it into a pattern, like a quilt. Each quilt pattern also indicates personal, domestic issues, and practices. This would appear remarkably cozy if it were not for the names of these quilting patterns, all of which reference problems, dangers, and the domestic guilt, secrecy, revelation and threat: "Jagged edge," "snake fence," "broken dishes," "secret drawer," and the myth forewarning revelations, exposés, women's guilt: "Pandora's box."

## GRACE'S FIRST PERSON NARRATIVE— TRUSTWORTHY TESTIMONY?

Grace's first person narrative opens the novel. A mixture of the almost childishly simple and the symbolic, it recalls James Joyce's *A Portrait of the Artist as Young Man*. But Atwood's novel presents us with a version of semi-fictionalized autobiographical prose delivered in a measured, constructed manner, hiding details, revealing others in the references and the images used, the occasional glimpses into a subtext indicating other versions and readings of events than those presented as the truth by Grace to anyone (including the reader). Like the peonies growing up through the gravel, an image, which Grace claims emerges following the death of her friend Mary Whitney, alternative versions are heard beneath Grace's testimony to us. These glimpses, creeping through fissures in the tale, gaps in Grace's public front, are in themselves, we suspect, much fuller than any testimony to the Governor's wife or other officials upon whose support she depends for her future welfare and possible release.

The opening paragraphs both hide and reveal, using various characteristics of the literary Gothic, first person narrative and imagery. Alternative, disruptive truths insinuate themselves like peonies through gravel. Grace herself acknowledges a barely repressed set of alternatives in her body language with her head tucked down, hands clasped, and her well fitting shoes, admitting that this restrained behavior is conducted with considerable discomfort and difficulty. "It's not easy being quiet and good, it's like hanging on to the edge of a bridge when you've already fallen over; you don't seem to be moving, just dangling there, and yet it is taking all your strength"(p. 5).

What Grace reveals in the opening paragraphs is an alignment between the peonies — hidden truths creeping through official versions, and the events of the day Nancy and Mr Kinnear died; Nancy's dress covered in pink rosebuds, her frightened gesture of putting her hand to her throat, vulnerable, upon seeing Grace and James McDermott. McDermott suggests cutting a throat, Nancy is startled, soon a victim, while Grace latterly knows how to protect herself, "I tuck my head down while I walk, keeping step with the rest" (p. 5), conforming, self protective, playing the game. But Grace's narrative is also revealing. She knows she must maintain a front, foresee the next move of those who control her, find ways of managing knowledge and truth for her own self protection. The better she behaves, the more she keeps her own counsel even from us as readers, the more likely she is to manipulate the inquisitiveness and missionary spirit, the salvation oriented generosity of the Governor's wife and her acquaintances. The better then can she play roles indicating to them her innocence and right to release. As readers, we might overlook these parallel versions at a first reading but as Grace's narration continues to repress and translate at least as much as it delivers, we return and reread, assembling the evidence, building a case, responding in our own way with judgements like those delivered by the formal official legal system, or the benefactors who wish her well.

Grace's first piece of narrative develops into the story she told Dr. Jordan, a tale recounted employing the language of dream recollection in which events and people shift, enact hoped for alternatives, indicate guilt and sadness at semi-hidden truths. In this version, Grace informs us, "this time it will all be different" because she will rescue Nancy, wipe the blood away and all will be well, order restored, with Mr. Kinnear arriving on his horse, coffee and the music filled peace of the evening following momentary mishaps in the garden. This positive version dissolves into recognition of what Grace represents as the real events, in which she figures as someone trapped by the situation and by a man. "I put my hands over my eyes because it's dark suddenly, and a man is standing there with a candle, blocking the stairs that go up; and the cellar walls are all around me, and I know I will never get out" (p. 6). Marvellously Freudian, this tale suggests entrapment, darkness, oppression through the cellar and the walls, sexual control of the looming man. In this version, she indicates that she tries to repress the sexual hold an unnamed man has on her, the unrecognized (for her) link between this hold and her unconscious, a wish to redress the wrongs of events only partly recalled. Petals and colors dissolving, the pieces cannot be reassembled

Freudian Dr. Jordan has read this sort of thing before. To him it indicates that Grace, misled by an unconscious set of sexual desires, overpowered by the will of a dark man, would really like to make things better, turn the clocks back. It does not fully indicate her involvement and could help suggest her vulnerability, even innocence, certainly her remorse and an eminently commendable desire to compensate. It could suggest she has grown morally during her incarceration, punishment has reformed her, and she is more self aware. But Grace's "This is what I told Dr. Jordan, when we came to that part of the story" (p. 6) betrays her subtle manipulation of Jordan's own frames of reference, constructing and retelling the tale he wants to hear. The emphasis on story highlights fictiveness, its constructed, undependable quality making us uneasy as readers. Used to trusting and seeing through the perspectives of reliable first person narrators, we hover on the edge of being taken in by Grace, aware she positions us as she positions Dr. Jordan. We recognize ourselves as gullible, ready to accept versions in which we can invest, which reinforce our beliefs and expectations. Those punishing the convicted similarly construct versions suiting their own prejudices. But for the reader, the ultimate truth, if there were to be such a thing, is revealed as always relative to the truth teller, context, and frame in which we tell and hear. Nothing is ever verifiable.

*Alias Grace* reveals itself in its first couple of pages as a real postmodernist text, constantly self-aware of its own constructedness, the relativity of any representation and version of what is real, what is history, and able to expose and enact performativity — the culturally constructed role play in which Grace excels.

Grace's narrative is partly about her dealings with identity and representation. While aware of the power of labels, Grace finds the title murderess both oppressive and attractive, seductive, hence the female imagery:

*Murderess* is a strong word to have attached to you. It has a smell to it, that word — musky and oppressive, like dead flowers in a vase. Sometimes at night I whisper it over to myself: *Murderess, Murderess.* It rustles, like a taffeta skirt across the floor. (pp. 22–23)

Looking at herself in the mirror, Grace assesses different version others have made of her ranging from "an inhuman female demon" to "an innocent victim of a blackguard forced against my will"(p. 23) asking, "How can I be all of these different things at once?"(p. 23), although she develops this diversity of representations in the novel. Her lawyer, MacKenzie, suggested she should appear rather stupid both to emphasize her innocence, and encourage others to believe she did not comprehend events. Against this he constructs versions of all witnesses as malicious liars.

## MADNESS, EVIL, AND TESTIMONY

In the Toronto Lunatic asylum, Grace is well aware of what is considered mad, although much of the madness around her is the result of drink and a desire to escape domestic abuse. Grace reflects on representations of her

Red hair of an ogre. A wild beast, the newspaper said. A Monster. When they come with my dinner I will put the slop bucket over my head and hide behind the door, and that will give them a fright. If they want a monster so badly they ought to be provided with one (p. 33).

Grace's relationship with Simon Jordan produces the story he wants to hear. Through discussion with her, she enables him to recount his own narrative. Grace acts as his confessor, a role reversal familiar to many women to whom men open their life stories. Simon Jordan attempts to reconstruct Grace's story, to analyze guilt or innocence, but she is seen to mold *her* tale to *his* needs, using *his* tale to her own ends:

He asks a question, and I say an answer, and he writes it down. In the courtroom, every word that came out of my mouth was as if burnt into the paper they were writing it on, and once I said a thing I knew I could never get the words back; only they were the wrong words, because whatever I said would be twisted around, even if it was the plain truth in the first place. (p. 68–9)

The feeling of being drawn out is both liberating: "hundreds of butterflies have settled all over my face, and are softly opening and closing their wings" (p. 68–9) and a constricting form of surveillance:

It's like being wakened suddenly in the middle of the night, by a hand over your face, and you sit up with your heart going fast, and no one is there. And underneath that is another feeling still, a feeling like being torn open; not like a body of flesh, it is not painful as such, but like a peach; and not even torn open, but too ripe and splitting open of its own accord. And inside the peach there's a stone. (pp. 68–69)

Grace's watchfulness indicates that she is perfectly aware of providing the doctor with manageable versions of her and her crimes. Tensing her body to release a story parallels that of tearing and cutting Nancy's body. Both are invasive, intrusive, painful. The peach Simon Jordon feels he has in front of him, Grace, signifies fruit, a woman to be nurtured and then used (as an information source on woman's madness). Grace nurses just a stone—a kernel of truth? A hard heart? She is perceptive about her power over him. Others, however, warn Simon of ways Grace, "an accomplished actress and a most practised liar" (p. 71) could overwhelm him. Sirens, mermaids, and mad, drowned Ophelia presage and enhance references of sexuality:

Many older and wiser heads have been enmeshed in her toils, and you would do well to stop your ears with wax, as Ulysses made his sailors do, to escape the sirens. She is as devoid of morals as she is of scruples, and will use any unwitting tool that comes to hand. (p. 71)

Her fits of madness are seen as performances. Hysteria and untrustworthiness are transferred onto the witness "worthy Mrs. Moodie," (p. 71) who is untrustworthy, believing "theatrical twaddle served up to her, provided it is pathetic enough" (p. 71). Hers is an "inaccurate and hysterical account" (p. 71).

We are no clearer about which is the truth, always conditional upon its source. Mrs. Moodie and McDermott both assess Grace as guilty, confessing. Reverend Verringer makes some fine distinctions:

"Since her return from the Asylum, however, you say she denies it."
    Reverend Verringer sips at his coffee. "She denies the *memory* of it,".
(p. 78)

Her voluntary confession (Voluntary confession of Grace Marks to Mr. George Walton, in the Gaol, on the 2nd of November, 1834, *Star and Transcript*, Toronto) recorded as epigraph to Chapter V, Broken Dishes, in fact is only a confession of her origins and family. Recorded in a newspaper, it could be fictionalized, elaborated, or curtailed. It certainly indicates localized racism, a cultural imperialism indicting the Irish immigrant experience as subordinate, strange, Other, potentially dangerous:

What it says at the beginning of my Confession is true enough. I did indeed come from the North of Ireland; though I thought it very unjust when they wrote down that *both of the accused were from Ireland by their own admission*. That made it sound like a crime, and I don't know that being from Ireland is a crime; although I have often seen it treated as such. (p. 103)

Grace's tale becomes one of local and wider politics, her story colludes with contemporary prejudice against Irish immigrants ". . . There is still a widespread feeling against Grace Marks; and this is a most partisan country. The Tories appear to have confused Grace with the Irish Question" (p. 80)

Her imagery of memories of Ireland, and landing in Canada, as broken plates, is both domestic, suitable for a maidservant and a woman, and suggests gradual piecing together in her recollections, testimonies, and narrative, indicating various ways in which readers might need to reconstruct information and evidence into a new whole. How very constructed and subject to interpretation is each version of a new pattern, a broken plate made good.

I don't recall the place very well, as I was a child when I left it; only in scraps, like a plate that's been broken. There are always some pieces that would seem to belong to another plate altogether; and then there are the empty spaces, where you cannot fit anything in. (p. 103)

There are other forms of deciphering patterns. Mary Whitney and Grace, imagining potential partners, peel an apple and throw the peel over one shoulder, spelling out a partner's initial — J. Apples suggest sexuality, forbidden knowledge, Adam and Eve. But here the old wives' tale of how to determine future husbands is seen as picky. Letters and clues are of accidents, myths — interactions — possibly as dependable as any testimony. Notably, the letter J could indicate James McDermott, Jamie Walsh, who testified against Grace at her trail and eventually becomes her husband, or Simon Jordon, a possibility not lost on the young psychoanalyst. Jordan's subconscious constructs visions stemming from ideas of the potential union of himself and Grace, although his conscious comments and actions are filled with formality and propriety.

### WOMEN'S LIVES AND ROLES

Attitudes towards her reflected contemporary ambiguity about the nature of women: was Grace a female fiend and temptress, the instigator of the crime and the real murderer of Nancy Montgomery, or was she an unwilling victim, forced to keep silent by McDermott's threats and by fear for her own life? (*Alias Grace*, Author's Afterward. p. 464)

Women's lives and roles are a favorite topic for Margaret Atwood. She poses questions about women's lives, constructions, and constraints in different contexts, using and interrogating different generic formats. Grace recognizes, then uses or rejects, the ways she is represented according to others' fantasies and worldviews. Similar self-awareness in *The Edible Woman* leads Marion, the protagonist, to identify herself as an item for consumption. The ending, in which Marion and a male friend finish off the head of a cake representing herself, is celebratory. In *The Handmaid's Tale*, a distopian vision of the future divides women into separate roles: worker, domestic, wife(for occasions), and handmaids, for procreation purposes. In a post-holocaust world where fertility is priceless, Offred the handmaid, nun-like, bored, oppressed, a kept brood mare valued only for breeding, risks her life to challenge the oppressive system.

Atwood's novels debate ways in which society and culture construct and represent women, exploring cultural myths, and moving between historical periods. *Alias Grace* appears to be a work of historical realism but highlights the tenuous nature of fixed, shared reality, and the inevitable and necessary fictionality of any representation. It focuses ways in which social roles constructed for women enable or prevent them telling their stories. Placing the tale in nineteenth century colonial Canada links *Alias Grace* with Atwood's other work dealing with identity and located in Canada. *Surfacing* explores wilderness versions of Canada set against North American intrusion, *Lady Oracle* and other texts including *The Robber Bride* are set in Toronto, and *Alias Grace* plunges us into colonial history, the Irish immigration to Canada, the harshness of life in a country newly settled with its cruel winters and its prejudices. This harshness is also seen both in Carol Shields's *Mary Swann*, which features a working class woman writer almost entirely hidden from notice and history, and Alice Munro's short stories of small town and rural relationship tragedies.

Grace, brought up in deprivation in Ireland, ships across in terrible conditions to Canada with her family. The death of her mother on the trip plunges the family into more poverty and suffering. Farmed out, under sized, her life is contrasted with that of pampered middle-class women. She is sharply observant of such personal and social contrasts, and of the constricting, contradictory lives of women in general. Jordan, who psychoanalyzes Grace, is characterized in terms of his beliefs and experiences of women's musculature, clothing and contemporary views of their frailty:

At least he isn't a woman, and thus not obliged to wear corsets, and to deform himself with tight lacing. For the widely held view that women are weak-spined and jelly-like by nature, and would slump to the floor like melted cheese if not roped in, he has nothing but contempt. While a medical student, he dissected a good many women—from the labouring classes, naturally—and their spines and musculature were on the average no feebler than those of men. (p. 73)

Grace's tale casts a light upon the lives led by working-class and middle-class women in the nineteenth century in Canada, and indeed in other colonies, and the United States and UK. It contributes to topical arguments about "the Woman Question" in the period when women intellectuals such as George Eliot, and U.S. Women's Temperance Movement campaigned for improved rights and a wider set of opportunities for women. These were set against the limited Victorian period constructions of women as either virgins or whores, their bodies straight-jacketed by corsets, their minds kept from study in case it affected their health (an argument we find in the medical journals of the period including the *"Lancet"* in the UK). Grace, allowed to work in the Governor's wife's parlor, is lucid on the contradictions facing contemporary women:

The visitors wear afternoon dresses with rows of buttons up their fronts, and stiff wire crinolines beneath. It's a wonder they can sit down at all, and when they walk, nothing touches their legs under the billowing skirts except their shifts and stockings. They are like swans, drifting along on unseen feet; or else like the jellyfish in the waters of the rocky harbour near our house. (p. 21)

It isn't only the jellyfish ladies that come. On Tuesdays we have the Woman Question, and the emancipation of this or that, with reform-minded persons. (p. 22)

These women are a mixture of the malleable, indefinable, creatures of the imagination, garbed as if disconnected from human construction and frailty, more like swans with unseen feet, but also rather brittle, artificial, distant, protected. The mix of ideal and severity captures exactly the Victorian construction of womanhood. Women are not expected to be natural, they are laced in to represent something idealized, virginal, delicate, and mythical. But Grace sees the falseness of this. Legs are hidden; the dangerous is repressed. Like jellyfish, they are delicate and translucent. In actuality, they could deliver a vicious sting. She sees the constraints and artifice, the potential for her own role play in enactments of womanhood constructed by this colonial society. At the nineteenth century's end in Canada, they discuss the New Woman's potential emancipation, education and equality. This locates interest in Grace at a volatile moment when women were seen (depending on your investment in the status quo) as potentially dangerously sexually, and intellectually alert, or ripe for recognition as men's equals.

Grace performs her role much like Mr. Jaggers' ex-murderess housekeeper in Dickens' *Great Expectations*. Gentle woman and murderess seem to fit ill together.

> although an object of fear, like a spider, and of charity as well, I am also one of the accomplishments. . . .
> The reason they want to see me is that I am a celebrated murderess. Or that is what has been written down. (p. 22)

She is a curiosity, dangerous, but tamed. In her case, the crime is still in question and the precise nature of her involvement utterly bound up with those changing views on women's potential, abilities, and rights.

### ROMANTIC FICTIONS AND FATAL ATTRACTIONS

*Alias Grace* is potentially a romantic fiction gone horribly wrong. If Grace was really in love with and goaded on by McDermott, she could pay for her collusion in his crimes with her life. If, in another reading, he killed Kinnear to secure Grace for himself, his choice sealed his fate.

The novel is one of fatal attractions (or near fatal attractions) and marks a clear link, in the Victorian and our own contemporary minds, between the (culturally, mythically, constructed, and invested in) sexual allure and fascination of women and sex, and its potentially deadly dangers. Cultural and psychological links between sex and death float into view in Simon Jordan's sea imagery-filled dreams and waking visions. Part of the fascination of Grace for others is her position, poised on the cusp of being either an innocent, wronged at the hands of a blackguard, or an embodiment of the wiles and toils of sirens seeking to deceive and cause the death of all—specifically the men involved.

In a transference which Julia Kristeva could elucidate, Simon Jordan and others offload onto women, here specifically Grace, their own desire, disgust, and terror at sex and their sexual longings and needs, demonizing the recipient, who is identified and blamed as the cause of such troubled and confused responses. Kristeva in *The Powers of Horror* (1982) recognizes the equation of women with the abject, the disgusting and rejected Other, tracing this sexual revulsion back to the infant's initial rejection of all that is not him, including faeces, the Mother, and latterly, women as representative cases. In a horror turn, women are seen as fascinatingly Other, sex and women as disgusting, engulfing, and potentially life threatening. Kristeva and Luce Irigaray's feminist psychoanalytic writings pinpoint the equation of sex and death and explain the roots in minds, practices, and media of such dominant conjunctions of women, sex and death.

Sex, love, and death, that Western Victorian partnership, figure differently for Grace and Lydia, the Governor's daughter, another focus for Simon Jordan's seething imagination, who bases her self image on indicators of fashion, Godey's ladies books, cultivating romantic dreams linking love, fidelity, and death. Lydia finds a friend's death worth cherishing, keeping her drowned friend's scarf. Romantic dreams are couched in a sado-masochistic longing for death. This straight-laced ostensibly moral society has a historically well documented seamy side. Sex and death, consistently linked in Grace's mind because of her past, for the Governor's daughters represent lasting romantic nostalgia, a fascination with artifice, manners, and romantic dreams. Women, delicate creatures in the public mind, are fascinated with the link between sex and death. They thronged to stand in the mud, illicitly thrilled to watch McDermott die. Mixing the sexual with the righteous they wanted to "breathe death in like fine perfume" (p. 28).

The tone of Grace's insightful record resembles that of Atwood's general narrative voice pointing out that advertisement of the trials of McDermott and Grace "bears a disturbing resemblance to a wedding invitation" (p. 59). For Simon Jordan, first sight of Grace fascinates because she resembles both a nun, a "maiden in a tow-ered dungeon" (p. 59) awaiting (his) rescue, and a witch to be burned at the stake. His responses are a typical but elaborated, clearly expressed (by the narrator) version of late Victorian man's views of woman: chaste, dangerous, exciting, to be rescued. This combination view allots him the exciting, multifaceted role of pun-isher, seducer, and the bringer of forgiveness. Simon dreams of corridors, his childhood ventures to touch the forbidden possessions of the maids in the attic at home. The Gothic imagery reveals fascination, fear of sexuality:

Simon is dreaming of a corridor. It's the attic passageway of his house, his old house, the house of his childhood; the big house they had before his father's failure and death. The maids slept up here. It was a secret world, one as a boy he wasn't supposed to explore, but did, creeping silent as a spy in his stocking feet. . . . With a shiver of excitement he'd examine their things, their forbidden things; he'd slide open the drawers, touch the wooden comb with two broken teeth, the carefully rolled ribbon; he'd rummage in the corners, behind the door: the crumpled petticoat, the cotton stocking, only one. He'd touched it; it felt warm. (p. 139)

Rummaging in the corners of the rooms and drawers of the maids, Simon allows his sexual energies free rein. The secret world of his boyhood is his parents' old house, a Jungian image which represents the self. In this house of hidden pleasure, versions of his self which he has repressed surface at night in dreams. The available, sensual maids and fetishistic items like their clothing and locked doors suggest repression, the sexually forbidden. Fascination and fear of the sexual as an exploration of self which makes men vulnerable, translates visually into locked doors, waiting girls, and language relating mermaids and the sea, offering a sexual drowning — loss of self, loss of life. In his dream the maids can swim leaving him to drown, victim of his (culpable) sexual needs.

Sitting on the edges of their narrow beds, in their white cotton shifts, their hair unbound and rippling down over their shoulders, their lips parted, their eyes gleaming. Waiting for him.

The door at the end opens. Inside it is the sea. Before he can stop himself, down he goes, the water closing over his head, a stream of silvery bubbles rising from him. In his ears he hears a ringing, a faint and shivery laughter; then many hands caress him. It's the maids; only they can swim. But now they are swimming away from him, abandoning him. He calls out to them, *Help me*, but they are gone. (p. 139)

Grace, too, is entrapped and drowning in her mind, memory, and tales. When she wonders what to keep of her own life, her versions of self, and of her relationship with McDermott, Grace produces for Simon Jordan her memories and a series of bizarre keepsakes. She rejects albums containing skewed or false evidence. The collection of mementoes from murder and Gaol sit uncomfortably next to a suggestion of her confusion based on love, "love in a mist;" defense a hapless innocent might use to differentiate herself from the guilty deceptions of man.

Nothing from McDermott, as I don't wish to remember him.

But what should a Keepsake Album be? Should it be only the good things in your life, or should it be all of the things? Many put in pictures of scenes and events they have never witnessed, such as Dukes and Niagara

Falls, which to my mind is a sort of cheating. Would I do that? Or would I be truthful to my own life.

A piece of coarse cotton, from my Penitentiary nightdress. A square of bloodstained petticoat. A strip of kerchief, white with blue flowers. Love-in-a-mist. (p. 382)

Simon Jordan's professional role is what makes him attractive to women. He holds power and knowledge, scientific information which could concern or cure them, or so they like to think, and he plays upon this. There is fascination with the macabre here, related to that fascination of the Victorians for collecting and labeling, for scientific experimentation involving grave robbing for specimens and for identifying characteristics of criminals through labeling physical features of physiognomy-phrenology. The secret of his allure is represented as a vampiric image of descent into the pit of the female, emerging with forbidden knowledge:

He has been where they could never go, seen what they could never see; he has opened up women's bodies, and peered inside. In his hand, which has just raised their own hands towards his lips, he may once have held a beating female heart.

Thus he is one of the dark trio—the doctor, the judge, the executioner—and shares with them the powers of life and death. To be rendered unconscious; to lie exposed, without shame, at the mercy of others; to be touched, incised, plundered, remade—this is what they are thinking of when they look at him, with their widening eyes and slightly parted lips. (p. 82)

This is sexually exciting, professional male power. Simon's medical knowledge is seductive. There is a salaciousness in women's readiness to trust this man. Our latter day knowledge of Foucault and his interpretations of relationships between power, knowledge, language, and sex expose these women who offer their vulnerability to young Simon Jordan, holder of arcane powers.

## WOMEN AND MADNESS: PSYCHOANALYSIS

Hysterics — These fits take place, for the most part, in young, nervous, unmarried women. . . . Young women, who are subject to these fits, are apt to think that they are suffering from "all the ills that flesh is heir to;" and the false symptoms of disease which they show are so like the true ones, that it is often exceedingly difficult to detect the difference.
— ISABELLA BEETON, *Beeton's Book of Household Management*,
1859–61 (p. 138)

Grace Marks, incarcerated in the Toronto Lunatic Asylum, exhibits several examples of such hysterical fits, one of which takes place when doctors attempt to examine and analyze her. But the very construction of Grace as hysterical or mad is itself culturally and historically inflected. Women, figured as too weak physically and feeble minded to be able to commit vile crimes, were seen as hysterical, out of control. Grace's own commentary on her fit when meeting the doctor suggests collusion with the personal safety and label of innocence offered by evidence of uncontrollable hysteria. If she is mad/hysterical, she cannot really be blamed.

Grace's story is also one of women and madness aligned with 1970s tales of women's breakdowns and breakthroughs, and contemporary (late nineteenth century) interest in psychoanalysis, in doctors' and patients' relationships. One thinks of Freud and Dora. In his psychoanalysis of Dora, a patient, Sigmund Freud interpreted her response to him through his sexually based psychoanalytical methods, finding that she transferred her affections to him, the analyst. Grace is seemingly a fit subject for study as a potentially violent, potentially innocent woman whose word is suspect. Simon Jordan stimulates her mind and their conversation with food and flowers, so she plays a game for him. He becomes so involved and fascinated with her that he relinquishes objectivity. Definitions of madness and sanity, of truth and of lies, circle this relationship.

Lindsay Duguid comments on the psychoanalytic elements, the layers of the novel which plumb the psyche and dreams and testify to contemporary fascination with accessing the dead. Atwood uses:

the most intense and poetic language to evoke extreme and terrifying mental states — sleep-walking and trances, amnesia and possession. Grace hears voices, and she has a recurring vision of Nancy crawling towards her with blood in her eyes, begging for mercy, a vision which is linked to a memory of scattered crimson petals. ( Duguid, 1996 p. 14)

Jordan attempts to win Grace around rather like one would a wild animal. Watching her quilt, he offers her daily different fruit and then root vegetables, hoping to plumb her subconscious "for a connection that will lead downwards: Beet — Root Cellar-Corpses, for instance; or even Turnip-Underground-Grave," revealing links between the moment, the offering of vegetables, and the deaths in the cellar where Nancy's body was discovered. Grace is too wily for this.

Grace hides much more than she reveals. Simon Jordan does not know what to make of it: "Every button and candle-end seems accounted for." He is particularly disturbed by her recollections of Mary Whitney, the lively young American who was her best friend until her unrecorded, early death following an illegal abortion. He "has an uneasy sense that the very plenitude of her recollections may be a sort of distraction, a way of drawing the mind away from some hidden but essential fact, like the dainty flowers planted over a grave." Grace knows Simon Jordan has no taste for flowers, yet she herself uses images of peonies to recall memories of Nancy's death. They are speaking different languages. As Grace's story gets closer to the day of the murder, her vague evasiveness turns into a prim refusal to discuss all things unladylike. This gives way to a terrified confusion which promises to be revealing—but is not.

The relationship between Grace and Simon Jordan is one fraught with Freudian influence. Jordan's own background as an only son in a household of lovely and potentially available young servant girls gave him some early sexual experiences which underlie his perceptions of and treatment of women more generally. In outlining his background in this way, Atwood highlights sexual tensions and sexual relationships of inequalities of power breeding in Victorian households. Power relations between master and servant, master and slave, lay behind any attachment to a servant girl. As a young boy, Jordon and other young men would have found the availability of older girls both terrifying and attractive. Sex then would be an uneasy association of constraint, presence and temptation, power and authority, the illicit, the rather dangerous(if found out)the denied, yet achieved pleasure. Once, caught out fondling a servant girl's shifts:

White-handed, as it were—he'd been fondling one of her shifts. She'd been angry with him, but couldn't express her anger of course, as she'd wanted to keep her position; so she'd done the womanly thing, and burst into tears. He'd put his arms around her to console her, and they'd ended up kissing. Her cap had fallen off, and her hair came tumbling down; long dark-blonde hair, voluptuous, none too clean, smelling of curdled milk. Her hands were red, as she'd been hulling strawberries; and her mouth tasted of them.

There were red smears afterwards, on his shirt, from where she'd started to undo his buttons; but it was the first time he'd ever kissed a woman, and he'd been embarrassed, and then alarmed, and hadn't known what to do next. (pp. 187–188)

The guilty pleasure he felt in this, augmented by actual excitement when Alice, the servant, returns his interest, produces a link between guilt, sex, pleasure, the illicit, and power. Looking at Lydia, Simon Jordan sees a young animal, fascinating, both hidden and available:

Simon is conscious of her white throat, encircled with a modest ribbon ornamented with a rosebud, as befits an unmarried girl. Through layers of delicate fabric, her arm presses against his. (p. 86)

His responses to servant girls transfer onto several women: his viewing of the Governor's daughter Lydia as an available "confection, and he doesn't wish to deprive himself of such an aesthetic pleasure too soon." She is to be dallied with (but not to get too involved). He is aware of the dangers of any relationship with his bony landlady. This parallels his increasing fascination with Grace who represents the attractiveness, the somewhat denied availability of the servant girls, and the illicit Other because of her status as murderess. Virginal Lydia is conflated with a dish and Parisian courtesans:

Lydia has burst into spring bloom. Layers of pale floral ruffling have sprouted all over her, and wave from her shoulders like diaphanous wings. Simon eats his fish — overdone, but no one on this continent can poach a fish properly — and admires the smooth white contours of her throat, and what can be seen of her bosom. It's as if she is sculpted of whipped cream. She should be on the platter, instead of the fish. He's heard stories of a famous Parisian courtesan who had herself presented at a banquet in this way; naked, of course. He occupies himself with undressing and then garnishing Lydia: she should be garlanded with flowers — ivory-coloured,

shell pink—and with perhaps a border of hothouse grapes and peaches.
(p. 193)

Simon is voyeur and devourer. Lydia is served up to admirers, a
young girl in a society of courtship where young women would be
handed over to the protection (and ownership) of a husband should
his assets prove him a fit match. Eliding Lydia with food and
Parisian courtesans shows the sexual, sensual, even sadistic (canni-
balistic) response lurking, repressed, beneath the formal. Waves,
wings, shell pink flowers equate Lydia with his fish lunch, and
seductive (but dangerous) mermaids; a vision Simon transfers to
Grace.

Any interpretation he might make of Grace's tale told during
visits as her psychoanalyst is affected by his personally charged,
unavoidable casting of her in a sexual light. Simon's repression and
gradual revelation of his fascination with Grace as both woman *and*
murderess emerges as he recalls his own history.

We see Grace constructed by Simon through images and recollections, interpretations of her past, her childhood, her influences
which could explain her actions. These are in the manner of psychoanalytic explanations which could eventually lead to insistence
on the lack of overt intent, the perceived helplessness of the perpe-
trator in the clutches of their own developed and inherited urges
and traits. Grace, untutored, plays to this. We perceive her role play
as we read and hear her responses to Jordon, seeing her choose
images and versions, words and inflections, which she know he will
be able to make much of. This behavior could be a genuine one of
recall, or an acting out of what she believes he wishes to hear.

An orchard. The cloth has tangled in the branches of a small tree covered
with green apples. He tugs it down and it falls across his face; and then he
understands that it isn't cloth at all but hair, the long fragrant hair of an

unseen woman, which is twining around his neck. He struggles; he is being closely embraced; he can scarcely breathe. The sensation is painful and almost unbearably erotic, and he wakes with a jolt. (p. 195)

Simon Jordon's dream of an orchard recalls Grace's tale of peeling an apple, throwing the peel over her shoulder and so discovering who she would marry, an old wives local folklore piece which here elides Eve, Adam, the Garden of Eden, and the forbidden apple connoting power, law and illicit sex. Internalized, these relations with repressed longing for Grace as ultimately dangerous, sexually fascinating woman, appear in Simon's dreams:

He knows he must still be asleep, because Grace Marks is bending over him in the close darkness, her loosened hair brushing his face. He isn't surprised, nor does he ask how she has managed to come here from her prison cell. He pulls her down — she is wearing only a nightdress — and falls on top of her, and shoves himself into her with a groan of lust and no manners, for in his dreams everything is permitted. His spine jerks him like a hooked fish, then releases him. He gasps for air. (p. 352)

But Simon's own confusions and weaknesses have here got the better of him: his bony landlady is the actual partner beside him.

It is not not Grace Marks who uncovers *her* secrets but Simon Jordan *his*: his salacious and repressed past, dreams and thoughts catching up with him. Even more unfortunately for Simon, neuroses from and dreams about maids transpose desire from Grace onto what he feels is a corpse, so directing the power relations, the sadism of his [repressed] version of what sexual relations are or could be. Her silence resembles death. His taking of the pulse on her neck converges the vampiric with the role of doctor. Grace, however, is deliberately prosaic, dealing with the everyday while also playing with the sexual power of her label:

"A murderess is not an everyday thing. As for my hopes, I save them for smaller matters. I live in hopes of having a better breakfast tomorrow than I had today." She smiled a little. "They said at the time that they were making an example of me. That's why it was the death sentence, and then the life sentence."

But what does an example do, afterwards? thought Simon. Her story is over. (p. 91)

He is wrong. Grace can construct a new life, new fictions beyond this relationship with her confessor/ psychoanalyst. Simon, sexually excited by her mixed homeliness and potential deadliness is thrilled to observe her sewing "completely natural and unbearably intimate," both homely and sensual, reminding Simon of his appointments with the maids. Thematically, sewing suggests what he has avoided, running a sewing machine factory (his mother's idea), and potential entanglements with those same maids. All versions of Grace's tale are represented as fabrications, but her story is far from sewn up. Moodie's tale is just as unreliable, as Reverend Veringer and Simon agree:

Mrs. Moodie is a literary lady, and like all such, and indeed like the sex in general, she is inclined to—"
    "Embroider," says Simon. (pp. 191–192)

Women, specifically Susannah Moodie and Grace, involved in the delicate pursuit of embroidery, could elaborate and redesign versions of events. Sewing suggests fabrication, construction, and castration. Grace, homely, sews her tale and stitches it all up. But Simon observes, "He felt as if he was watching her undress, through a chink in the wall; as if she was washing herself with her tongue, like a cat" (p. 91).

*Murderess, murderess*, he whispers to himself. It has an allure, a scent almost. Hothouse gardenias. Lurid, but also furtive. He imagines himself breathing it as he draws Grace towards him, pressing his mouth against her. *Murderess*. He applies it to her throat like a brand. (p. 388–389)

Revelations fascinate him, create ownership—of the woman, of the truth. Flower imagery provides a link with Grace's own such imagery. For Simon Jordan this is a heady opiate, overwhelming and dulling the senses, while for Grace it indicates truths blossoming, blooming through the controlled (concrete, fixed) versions of events. Simon's application of the label "murderess" to Grace's throat like a brand reminds us of the hypocrisy of another tightly reined, moralistic American society in Hawthorne's *The Scarlet Letter* which vilified adulteress Hester Prynne. Versions of Grace are products of her morally split, hypocritical, class ridden, and sexually repressed society. She is branded here to indicate her guilt, but it indicts her society also.

Our insights into Simon Jordan's motives and the ways in which his own experience influences his interpretations provide us with a balance of testimony and interpretation in context. We are not anywhere nearer any version of truth, but more aware of how different contexts and casts of mind, different periods, and different individuals construct and affect readings of events and of motivations. Seemingly objective and informed by science, all are affected by the interpreter's subjectivity. That Simon Jordan will never really understand the imagination and worldview of Grace is clear from her use of flower imagery—peonies creeping or bursting from concrete—and what we are told of him, "he has never known much about flowers" (61). It is a multi-layered text. The novel's network of imagery reveals interpretations and difficulties of communication.

## THE SUPERNATURAL, SPIRITUALISM

"Gentlemen," DuPont begins, "I am at a loss. I have never had an experience quite like this before. The results were most unexpected. As a rule, the subject remains under the control of the operator." He sounds quite shaken.

"Two hundred years ago, they would not have been at a loss," says Reverend Verringer. "It would have been a clear case of possession. Mary Whitney would have been found to have been inhabiting the body of Grace Marks, and thus to be responsible for inciting the crime, and for helping to strangle Nancy Montgomery. An exorcism would have been in order." (p. 405)

*Alias Grace* explores contemporary fascination with the fantastic, the supernatural and spiritual worlds, Victorian supernatural occurrences such as table-tapping and mediumship. While Grace's doctor explains her actions as symptoms, she uses contemporary dependency on the supernatural to suggest that any evil resulted from possession by her dead friend, Mary Whitney, her alter ego or doppelganger. This Gothic twinning or mirroring image also suggests the duplicitous nature of Grace herself, and the many sides to her tale.

Margaret Atwood focuses on spiritualism in her earlier *Lady Oracle* which deals with issues of romance and identity. In *Alias Grace*, she uses the contemporary fascination with the spiritual to explore ways in which Grace was represented or could be represented and understood according to the beliefs of the time. Seeking proof of afterlife, and of a spiritual dimension insisted on in church and religious ceremonies, ordinary people flocked to mediums and spiritualists for contacts with loved ones, and beyond the grave evidence. They were dependant upon faith, proofs, and evidence of the everyday, factual kind. Grace makes the most of these beliefs.

Jeremiah the peddler, from whom Grace and others buy buttons and other items, reappears as a spiritualist towards the end of the novel. He emerges again later when Grace has married Mr. Walsh, more respectable, his hair dyed and beard trimmed, in another guise. They wink at each other, collusive

A slightly earlier age would easily have labeled Grace's mixed responses and claims about Mary Whitney as a clear case of possession. This transitional age is less sure.

### FORMS OF WRITING—VERSIONS OF THE "TRUTH"

*Alias Grace* presents us with several versions of events, from individual testimonies to newspaper reports. As such, it is a historiographical metafiction like John Fowles' *The French Lieutenant's Woman*, Pat Barker's *Regeneration*, and Julian Barnes' *Flaubert's Parrot*. Like them, it comments on the constructedness of versions of the historical past, showing us ways these are constructed in different kinds of storytelling or writing. Historiographical metafiction works by highlighting how versions are dependent on who produces them, how they are passed down to us, how edited, how interpreted. The partiality and bias of versions of the past become obvious and the text forces us to question how or if we could ever know either the truth of this particular set of incidents or of anything in the recorded past. Different versions of Grace's tale derive from different peoples' prejudices. Ballad, newspaper, and the Governor's wife's scrapbook of the lives and horrors of criminals illustrate the translation and stereotyping of cases and a late nineteenth century fascination with guilty, evil minds. Ballads give us common myths, tales embellished by romance and horror, the supernatural, tales embedded in folklore, which turn into local myths to warn others about forms of misbehavior and their consequences. Newspaper reports indicate bias of the writers, limited access to what are considered the facts of a case, representing facts as if fixed entities.

McDermott . . . was morose and churlish. There was very little to admire in his character. . . . (He) was a smart young fellow, so lithe that he would run along the top of a zigzag fence like a squirrel, or leap over a five-barred gate, rather than open or climb it. . . .

Grace was of a lovely disposition and pleasant manners and may have been an object of jealousy to Nancy. . . . There is plenty of room for the supposition that instead of her being the instigator and promoter of the terrible deeds committed, she was but the unfortunate dupe.

—WILLIAM HARRISON, "Recollections of the Kinnear Tragedy," written for the *Newmarket Era*, 1908 (p. 183)

Undependable as sources of truth, newspapers seem to need to find a typical, guilty party, a usual (male) suspect; and an innocent or deceased woman. McDermott might be known to lie—but we hear Grace do so also.

"The murder of Thomas Kinnear, Esq. And of his housekeeper Nancy Montgomery at Richmond Hill and the trials of Grace Marks and James McDermott and the hanging of James McDermott at the new gaol in Toronto, November 21st 1843" records an event. It is a ballad titled like a newspaper report. However, like other such ballads including those of Thomas Hardy and *The Runaway Slave at Pilgrim's Point* by Elizabeth Barrett Browning, themselves built upon traditional ballads such as *"Oh No John,"* this one both privileges certain versions of events, and couches these readings within traditional formulae involving working-class protagonists pitted against the rich: "Grace Marks she was a serving maid;" "Now Thomas Kinnear was a gentleman/and a life of ease led he." This underlines social injustice in such inequalities, partly explaining a turning to crime. Traditionally, ballads focus on social inequalities, on lives of crime, love won and lost, tragedy, intermingling social critique with religious belief in Fate, a metaphysical mirroring, the injustice or justice of the gods influencing any managing of rewards or punishments (some fair, some unfair. Humans are largely helpless). McDermott speaks here alone, as does Nancy, who begs for her life and that of Kinnear. Grace appears as bold and duplicitous. The ballad enables those who have had no voice to speak for themselves, filling in imagined details, motives, events, and casts it all as a love story so that "From Nancy's grave there grew a rose; and from Thomas Kinnear's a vine/They grew so high they intertwined/and thus these two were joined."

But Grace will pass her life wearily in gaol until she goes to Heaven and repents. The ballad is formulaic and much neater than the versions we read. The only little ironic element is the dissection of McDermott after hanging, at the university, which links the events with scholarship (again in a balladic, mythic format) reminding us that we are still seeking after truth.

Susanna Moodie provides contemporary testimony on Grace, seeing her as suffering "hopeless sorrow" but, with her long curved chin, "a cunning, cruel expression" and "Grace Marks glances at you with a sidelong stealthy look; her eye never meets yours, and after a furtive regard" (*Life in the Clearings*, 1853, quoted p. 20). Set next to Emily Brontë's supportive, gentle poem about a prisoner, the two records provide a balanced response to Grace—but leave readers wondering which would be the more appropriate. Fascination with fixing predominates. Collecting records of evil:

The Governor's wife cuts these crimes out of the newspapers and pastes them in; she will even write away for old newspapers with crimes that were done before her time. It is her collection, she is a lady and they are all collecting things these days, and so she must collect something, and she does this instead of pulling up ferns or pressing flowers, and in any case she likes to horrify her acquaintances. (p. 26)

The Governor's wife's scrapbook is part of the memorabilia of criminal activities of the time. Her fascination with fixing, knowing, collating, and presenting items concerned with criminal cases, particularly of Grace Marks, shows a gruesome mixed desire to understand the criminal mind and its actions, and to wallow in mementoes of evil, believing that by pasting them into an annotated scrapbook they are fixed, understood, controlled. Phrenology, which studies the criminal mind and criminal tendencies by identifying physical types — in particular lumps, bumps and shapes of the head — springs from the same pseudo-scientific fixation. Pickling McDermott's head preserves it for examination and scientific purposes, but it is also a keepsake.

"They cut off his head," says Miss Lydia in a lower voice. "McDermott's. They have it in a bottle, at the University in Toronto."

"Surely not," says Simon, disconcerted afresh. "The skull may have have been preserved, but surely not the entire head!"

"Like a big pickle," says Miss Lydia with satisfaction. (p. 89)

The Victorian need to categorize and catalogue in order to name and know the world is based upon fashionable forensics among other focused, biased categorizing systems. The novel enables us to perceive how different versions of lives can be constructed and represented. It becomes a palimpsest, a layered text representing facts, historical detail, multi-layered, and imaginative versions and a variety of fictional constructions. We are aware of how different genres and takes on life and history force us to read things in certain ways, how the beliefs, representations, and values of a particular time condition responses and histories passed down to us.

Atwood in *Alias Grace*, and the later *The Blind Assassin*, locates the reader at the center of a whole variety of different ways of trying to pin down, articulate, and write up fact, memory and history, showing it always to be partial, dependent on subjectivity, point of view, the motive for recollection and record, and the format and location for such record.

Many versions of Grace's story appear. Her own narrative is riddled with articulated agents of artifice, the undependability of versions of "the truth" and Grace's deliberate fine tuning to suit her listener. The novel also questions the representation and construction of women's lives.

Atwood's employment of "Canadian Gothic" enables such concerns to be intertwined, different constructions and representations stitched into the emerging and still partially hidden patterns of Grace's narrative, of the quilt she sews, the quilt of the novel, and of the text as a whole. Gothic imagery, the house of the self and soul, alter egos, patterning and interweaving, snakes, vines, sexual/death laden dreams and visions, cellars and root vegetables, fissures and cracks, flowers growing up through cracks, hint at dangerous repression, duplicity which connote the construction and representation of identity and self, of women, and of history and record. Grace's own quilt pattern of the Tree of Paradise self consciously combines all of these motifs. Her quilt rewrites the Biblical tale, equating good and evil, exonerating Eve who only behaves naturally:

On my Tree of Paradise, I intend to put a border of snakes entwined; they will look like vines or just a cable pattern to others, as I will make the eyes very small, but they will be snakes to me; as without a snake or two, the main part of the story would be missing. (pp. 459–460)

Significantly, the pattern will contain triangular pieces of Mary Whitney's petticoat, Grace's prison nightdress and Nancy's own dress.

I will embroider around each one of them with red feather-stitching, to blend them in as a part of the pattern.

And so we will all be together. (pp. 459–460)

Like the crime and its judgement, Simon Jordan and the quilt, we too are stitched up by Grace.

# 3

# The Novel's Reception

**A**lias Grace has received a great deal of critical attention since its publication. Two main areas of interest recur in critical comment. One is concerned with historically contextualizing the representation and treatment of women, looking at how Grace herself is constructed by the confusions of a period which saw women as either virgins or whores, guiltless and pure, or demonic. Another concentrates on how the novel problematizes ways in which people and historical records are obsessed with the impossible task of fixing, articulating, proving history, and the facts of any events. Both recognize quilting as the novel's central metaphor for making patterns and versions, for women's creativity, and the construction of identity.

Reviewers identify both Alias Grace's Victorian novel strategies and ways in which it replicates the problems of such texts. The desire to fix history, reality, and events, popular in the Victorian period, is problematized in our own. With "false memory syndrome" we cannot rely on individual memory. With amnesia and faked amnesia, witness accounts and confessions are dubious evidence. The context in which information is received and interpreted is fundamental.

The tale is seen as sensational, the representation of Grace mired in nineteenth century misogyny, rich in humanity; a fascinating story ultimately refusing closure. Reviewers perceive the Victorian qualities of the novel, its interest in the psychological, its construction and representation of women, its dealing with the lack of dependability of historical records and memories of all kinds. Some reviewers take a feminist approach, noting the context in which Grace is constructed and represented, while others focus on Gothic qualities. Most deal with the historical constructedness and artifice, the potential deception of testimony and memory. Some include interviews with Atwood. While acknowledging her insistence that tales she tells do not resemble her own life experiences, interviewers and reviewers alike seek similar traits (role play, construction of identity), showing her constructing a public self, aware of representing a Canadian consciousness, Canadian issues, locations and history. They celebrate her language play, her irony.

## THE HISTORICAL AND CANADIAN

The novel is a record of the times, but also treats universal issues, as Lindsay Duguid points out:

There is an attractive portrait about such things as a postage reform, the coming of the railroad and the fashion for bustles. What really interests Atwood is a deeper, more timeless (or perhaps more modern) enquiry into relations between men and women, masters and servants, bodies and civilisation. (Duguid, 1996, P. 14)

There is an equally accurate record of ways in which people of the time turned to alternative sources of information and insight- mesmerism, hypnotism, seances, and the like in "crude theories of 'neuro-hypnotism', unleashing terrible demons." The novel could be a tale of possession. Focusing on its spiritualism as a product of its period, Moore (1997) comments that

This is the age of scientific disciplines and unbridled mysticism — studies of the brain and drawing room table-rapping seances, electromagnetic therapies and mesmerism. This is a novel about gender and power and the upheaval of superstition in the face of what may or may not be provable theory.

Simon Jordan represents developing thought and practices in psychoanalysis. Links with contemporary "false memory" syndrome and states of amnesia engages twenty-first century readers. However, amnesia is very easy to fake. Atwood refuses to reveal.

This is a postmodernist text and as such utilizes intertextuality to convince contemporary readers of the tone and texture of the period. Peter Kemp (1996) identifies intertextual references of Victorians Tennyson, Browning, and Morris, noting Atwood conjures up not only terrors of the period but its zeitgeist — the way it lives and breathes, and its imagination (largely Gothic):

Place, too, is conjured up with pressing immediacy. The way in which fustiness and rawness mingle in the mid-nineteenth-century provincial Canadian society is pungently conveyed — not least in scenes where Atwood exercises her flair for throwing a Gothic sheen over the everyday: furniture in the governor's wife's parlour is done out in "the colours . . . of the inside of the body — the maroon of kidneys, the reddish purple of hearts, the opaque blue of veins, the ivory of teeth and bones."

Margaret Atwood's achievement in writing what appears and sounds like a nineteenth century novel, contains "ponderous wealth of historical detail and research," a crash course in Victorian culture: elementary discourses on the middle class's passion for spiritualism, its quasi-religious faith in progress, its mounting discomfort with the gap between the theology and science (Prose, 1996) and Gothic twists. Paradoxically, this mixture entertains as it "evokes the high Victorian mode, spiced with the spooky plot twists and playfully devious teases of the equally Gothic — the literary styles of the period in which the book is set."

Comparing *Alias Grace* to work by Charlotte Brontë, Daphne du Maurier, and the Canadian Alice Munro, Prose emphasizes the authentic creation of a voice for Grace, providing insights into the daily lives of the servant classes. This laundry excerpt, Atwood tells us, springs from her own experiences:

"When we had a wash hanging out and the first drops began to fall, we would rush out with the baskets and gather all in as quickly as we could, and then haul it up the stairs and hang it out anew in the drying room, as it could not be allowed to sit in the baskets for long because of mildew. . . . The shirts and the nightgowns flapping in the breeze on a sunny day were like large white birds, or angels rejoicing, although without any heads. But when we hung the same things up inside, in the gray twilight of the drying room, they looked different, like pale ghosts of themselves hovering and shimmering there in the gloom."

Prose misses the duplicity of Grace's everyday statement. This one about a washday is riddled with decapitated creatures and ghosts so we sense Grace is haunted by the murders, violent urges, and madness which she never acknowledges in her first person narrative.

Atwood's deliberate use of the recorded weight of history, evidence, and research which accumulate around a historical event and/or person is not pretentious scholarship. Recreation of the weight of the research detail needed to contextualize and interpret Grace and the murders deliberately indicates that ponderous excess can never bring us or any other researchers closer to what really happened, what the "truth" is.

Catherine Pepinster (1996) describes *Alias Grace* as historical fiction, positioning Atwood as a Canadian writer moving easily between the worlds of bush and city. Atwood's own continuing determination to identify and place Canadian Literature on the map pays off in Pepinster's review which recognizes and places this novel in terms of the work of other great Canadian writers:

Canada—the two-sided nation of Francophone Quebecers and Anglophone Ontarians—reflects the light and dark of both Grace and Atwood's characters. Atwood has lived in both parts of Canada, in commercial Toronto and northern Quebec, part of the mythology of the North that all Canadians are steeped in. The North is the place where you find yourself, and get in touch with nature.

The days are long gone when Canada could be written off as a literary outback.

### FEMINISM AND THE TREATMENT OF WOMEN

Fascination with the murderess tinges our investigations, Atwood's, and those contemporary to the historical events. Grace is a puzzling case. On one hand, if she has been the vulnerable, naïve member of a love tangle with a more powerful, persuasive, duplicitous man, she is herself a victim both of his promises which lead her to involvement in murder, and of the contemporary labeling of women who commit crimes as mad. On another hand, she could be a devious testifier, embodying conventional versions of women's destructive sexuality. Equal partner in the crimes McDermott commits, she would be a worse criminal than he. She refuses guilt, persuades others, particularly Simon Jordan, of her innocence, and succeeds in reinforcing Jordan's desires and terrors of women's sexuality. In this reading, Grace is a siren, attracting with her stories; drawing Jordan in to destroy him.

Atwood's quarrels with second wave feminism's often rather simplistic take on gendered representations and politics were more an issue in her earlier works. Atwood has moved on. Actually, post-second wave feminism has moved on too. She argues:

"Every woman who appeared in the early seventies was called a feminist writer. Suddenly we noticed women in a different way than they'd been noticed before—as neurotic, with their heads in the oven or strange spinsters. I am a writer who writes for people to who read books." (Atwood in Pepinster, 1996, p. 9)

Carol Angier (1996) takes a late twentieth century feminist perspective, positioning Atwood's novel among her earlier works in terms of treatment of women, specifically focusing on the interaction between Simon Jordan and Grace as she answers (or evades) his questions. *Alias Grace* is a "Gothic tale of sex and class," focusing on the love between Kinnear and Montgomery, the supposed love between Grace and McDermott, and ways in which men construct and represent Grace. Atwood's tale resembles myths, fairytales, and nineteenth century texts such as *Jane Eyre*. Atwood, engaging with sex and psychology, constructions and representations of women, has Simon Jordan seeing Grace as a maiden, incarcerated in a prison/tower, needing rescue. But this is a male construct: the maiden reveals herself as a self-possessed woman. "This is the key to her story, which is about the way men project their sexual desires and fears onto women, and call them mad and evil."

Lindsay Duguid also recognizes the popular Victorian myth of beautiful, wronged, and trapped woman, filtering out contemporary, topical fascination with sex and death. That we never find out the full truth is crucial. This feminist reading identifies both victimized woman and sly feminists:

> The ruined women in the story—Grace's friend Mary, who dies of a botched abortion; Kinnear's mistress, Nancy, slain by McDermott (or possibly Grace); Jordan's laudanum-sipping landlady—suggests that Grace's undoubted slyness may be part of an effective defence against those who have power over her: father, master, lawyer, gaoler, doctor. Women are not delicate angels of the house, picturesque and innocent victims. (Duguid, 1996 p. 14)

The Victorian period constructed and represented women as virgins or whores but the "angel in the house" image fitted ill with that of woman as potential murderess. Grace, being young and pretty, just sixteen at the time of the murders, could easily be cast as an innocent victim and romantic dupe of McDermott's wiles. She was certainly a character in the imagination of those around her; the religious fanatics who invited Simon Jordan to analyze her, perhaps proving her innocence, and the spiritualists, fascinated by her tales of possession by the ghost of her dead friend, Mary Whitney. People trusted in pseudo-science and sciences alike. Psychoanalysis, a new science, could judge Grace as innocent, duped, or confused, a victim of her own inner psychological problems. Alternatively, she could reveal the true horrors of events. Simon Jordan, with a past of secret visits to and relations with servant girls at home, and some extremely morally dubious dreams and memories, would not be a reliable witness. He is an expert affected by his own experiences and beliefs, however suppressed.

Recently, *Alias Grace* has been compared with the range of Atwood's work in terms of issues of identity, Canadian qualities, and women's roles. Most critical books on Atwood came out before *Alias*

*Grace* was published but one by Stein (2000) relates the novel to her earlier works. Late twentieth century critics, likening *Alias Grace* to the prize-winning *The Blind Assassin* (2000), focus on the unreliability and jigsaw puzzle nature of contrasting historical records with testimony, on the Canadian qualities, constraints both political and historical, on women's identities, their roles. Like *Alias Grace*, *The Blind Assassin* is also partly personal testimony, partly a layered text of documentary, journalistic, literary, and historical records. It too highlights the palimpsestic nature of our histories, both public and personal.

Both texts are postmodernist, focusing on the fragmentary nature and the undependability of history and memory; both use intertextuality, problematizing "reality" and the "self" as unitary. In keeping with Atwood's incorporation of and contribution to the development of popular fictional genres, themselves cultural indeces, both novels incorporate elements of popular fiction to make their case. *Alias Grace* is crime or detective fiction, a horror novel plumbing the psyche and revealing trauma through imagery and memory. So, too, is *The Blind Assassin*, although the later novel also incorporates science fictions and a steamy romance.

## FORM AND STRUCTURE

Identifying metaphors of both quilts and keepsake albums, Peter Kemp (1996) signals ways in which the contours of patchwork reveal Grace's feelings, patch together versions of events, refusing a final reading. A local clergyman protests, "We cannot be mere patchworks." But the patchwork quilt is Atwood's structural image for the novel *and* Grace's personality. What she reveals and hides have sexual and bodily overtones: "Grace, an expert at making quilts, notes how their flaring colours signal the importance of the bed as the place of domestic dramas: births, sex, sickness, death, dreams, nightmares" (Kemp, 1996, p. 11).

Quilting becomes a way of prescribing varied textures of records in the novel. Other critics note the alignment of the novel's structure with its feminist and psychological focus. Atwood tempering and tampering with Susanna Moodie's versions gives us guilty, Gothic, Grace Marks. She unearths contemporary versions, measuring them against Moodie's questionable elaborations, formed from reading the newspapers: she was very ready to see a "cunning, cruel expression . . . a sidelong, stealthy look . . . coloured by her penchant for Dickens at his most Gothic and for Harrison century best-sellers" (Mantel, 1996). Faced with the issue of record and imaginings, "Grace herself proposes a metafictional solution: 'When you are in the middle of a story it isn't a story at all, but only a confusion' " (Duguid 1996, P. 14). Confusion turns to patchwork, to quilting metaphors throughout the novel indicating the patching and muddling together of versions of truth, recall, imaginative reconstructions, lies, and the actual structure of the novel itself. Maureen Freely (1996) takes such a quilting and recall route, identifying Atwood's interest as lying less in changing the few known facts. Rather: "The art is in the pattern she forms with them, and the imaginative possibilities are in the story's gaps. Her star invention is an American doctor and protopsychologist named Simon Jordan."

Quilt patterns, key to Grace's tale, her untold subtext, also indicate Simon Jordan's alternative agenda in unraveling Grace's story. As a son without an inheritance he must make a name for himself as a "master plumber of the criminal subconscious" (Freely, 1996, p. 18) to attract necessary investors, but not at any cost. "He still sees himself as being in the truth business. He is determined to get Grace to speak for herself" (Freely, 1996, p. 18). As Grace's own version of the story is constructed before us, Simon Jordan's life seems spiralling out of control "his life outside the sewing room has become a nightmare mirror-image of the story he has been record-ing" (Freely, 1996, p. 18)—leaving readers trying to piece it all together as "Atwood charts his descent from absentminded charity into erotic madness and unprofessional conduct with her usual glee. Despite his old-fashioned clothing, he is one of her stock characters. The bleary-eyed landlady is another regular, as is Grace."

Hilary Mantel (1996) also recognizes that Atwood, like Grace, is an expert quilter, illustrating how we patch together versions of reality and events:

Our experience, our very consciousness, is fragmented and can be rear-ranged, she suggests; your perception of the past is likewise a thing of shreds and patches . . . 500 pages are shaken out and the dazzling design shows, in all the glory of its pattern, texture and color.

What is quilted and patched together? History and fantasy, but the boundaries are unclear. Mantel traces Grace's origins in a poor Irish family, her mother dead on the crossing to Canada, her escape from a brutal father into the constraints of domestic servitude, taking up with good tempered, pretty Nancy who offers her a job. Grace, Mantel suggests, perceives Mr. Kinnear's household is not as straightforward as it seems. He crosses boundaries in his relationship with Nancy, who has become his mistress, and for whom he buys gold ornaments and jewelery. Grace perceived the boundary crossing. Perhaps something awakens in her—her sexuality, her desires for a better life. Location on the edge of the town, the forest, indicates that it is possible to stray over location and behavioral boundaries. Nothing is fixed. Both behavior and testimony are flex-ible, depending on point of view. Everything Grace says needs tempering and scrutinizing because she presents so many variations of events and of herself. Piecing together her basic beliefs—lack of sympathy for victims, for example, helps us construct a more dependable version of both events and Grace's culpability, but we will never know an absolute truth.

LeClair (2001) uses the language of seduction, guilt, and quilting, seeing the writing characterized by a "coiled discipline," aligning form with content arguing it is *"criminally seductive.* And since the murderess, Grace Marks, tells much of the tale, she becomes the most telling displacement yet of Atwood the subversive artist and ideological outlaw." While Margaret Rogerson compares quilting structures to narrative voice shifts:

Significant narratological variation occurs when Grace comes to the account of the actual murders. The voice that she uses on this occasion is not her own. Not only does she speak in third-person dialogue, but, in addition, the words that she utters were scripted by others. (Rogerson, 1998, p. 14)

What is seen at any one time depends on whether the pattern of Grace's history is read by looking at dark or light patches in her quilt. Her marriage to a man whose testimony helped put her behind bars is questionable. They sleep under a second-hand and potentially unlucky Log Cabin quilt: a comment on their new life. We cannot interpret Grace's tale because she uses the idiolect of quiltmakers since "Grace has asserted the wholeness of her life story in the Tree design, but, because she speaks in a quiltmaker's idiolect, her meanings are unclear, perhaps even to herself. Both the novel and the album quilt that Grace is planning on its final pages remain teasingly unfathomable."

We can never decide finally on Grace's guilt, not merely because versions vary, but also because hers is a "Bonnie and Clyde" scenario, fascinating. Grace's culpability is decided according to the habits of popular culture since "Usually opinion is undivided about the man—he dunnit—and divided about the woman. Was she the demon instigator? Was she playing Bonnie to his Clyde? Or was she a terrorized bystander only peripherally involved, fleeing out of terror for her own life" (Wiley, 2001). Comparing the story to other notorious cases, Lizzie Borden who killed her family, serial murderer Ted Bundy who mutilated and killed women, and the more recent OJ Simpson trial, Wiley details public fascination, recognizing the Kinnear love rectangle provides much interest for contemporary readers. It is no more complex in origins than an episode of Rikki Lake or Jerry Springer but more fatal in its consequences. Atwood says:

Somebody suggested that I try turning it into a play, and I did try, but I'm not really a playwright, and it didn't really work out. I was still just using Moodie's version. Time went by, lots of time went by, and I started working on the current novel, and at that point I went back to the historical record, such as it was, and found out that Susanna Moodie in fact had not remembered very accurately. (in Wiley, 1996)

Romantic fiction, psychoanalytic recall, testimony, and false memory jostle together in the versions offered by Grace Marks and the novel. Simon Jordan's conversations with Grace provide a romantic fiction reading for Christopher Lehmann-Haupt (1996) who believes readers expect Simon and Grace to fall in love because of the intensity of their time together while Atwood uses the sensationalist aspects of the Grace Marks' case to attract interest and readership. Grace is a Scheherazade, compelling Simon Jordan to listen, simultaneously enthralling readers. It is a powerful story echoing recurrent concerns: identity, gender relations, power. Searching for the truth, a scientific quest dependent upon underpinning belief that there is such as thing as a fixed and discoverable truth in the first place, is fundamentally undermined here. Simon, keen to open his own asylum, is sent by Grace's supporters to "open her up like an oyster" (Lehmann-Haupt, 1996).

This (thwarted) romantic fiction reading of the relationship between Simon Jordan and Grace Marks misses the voyeuristic, rather
lascivious subconscious responses Jordan develops while psychoan-
alyzing Grace. Grace herself, talking of quilting, imagines The
Garden of Eden and Tree of Paradise as patterns she can reproduce.
This suggests both dangers of searching after forbidden knowledge,
and ways in which Western society consistently indicts women as
causing all evil.

## ATWOOD AND GRACE

Atwood comments on the influence Grace Marks had in her imagination after reading about her case in Susanna Moodie's version.
This did not entirely fit with documentary details of the time, nor
did it seem dependable given the context of views about and treatment of women in the late Victorian period:

Years passed and Grace Marks continued to wander around in my head. I
wrote a script about her for a television play. More time passed and she
kept insisting on being given a fuller hearing, so I began to write this novel.
Was Grace Marks the cunning female demon many considered her to be —
or was she simply a terrorized victim? I began researching, not only the
murder case but life in Victorian times. Every major element in the book
was suggested but something in the writing about Grace and her times,
however suspect such writing might be; in gaps left unfilled, I was free to
invent. Since there were a lot of gaps, there is a lot of invention. (Atwood,
*Reader's Companion*, 1996)

The novelist is a historian and so is Simon Jordan. So indeed are
we as readers constructing fuller pictures of events in context, taking
into account the interpretations of others and what influences these

interpretations. It is a multi-layered text with a multi-layered interpretation.

Ironically, the comfortable bed quilt—metaphor for patching
together versions of the truth; actual structural form of the novel—
is not so safe in Grace Marks' or Atwood's hands. Marketing *Alias
Grace* resembles *Basic Instinct*, hinting at the deadly:

The bound galley lists the publishers' marketing strategies for *Alias Grace*:
multi-city author tour, a video of the novelist available to reading groups
and a bookstore display featuring an *"Alias Grace* quilt inspired by Margaret
Atwood". . . . in the privacy of her own home she'll chuckle at anyone who
wants to sleep under an *Alias Grace* quilt. It may have been sewn by a
stone-cold killer. (LeClair, 2001)

# 4

# The Novel's Performance

**A**lias Grace was a best-selling novel on both sides of the Atlantic and all round the world. Published simultaneously by a variety of publishers — Bloomsbury, Chivers, Random/Bantam (UK), Vintage and Anchor (United States), Virago (UK) and Mclelland Stuart (Canada) in hardback and paperback, its sales figures are considerable. Bloomsbury (UK) who published the novel in hardback to date have sold 80,000. McLelland Stuart report 130,000 sold in 1997 alone. The novel reached number seven on the *Guardian* bestseller list in 1997, which is no mean feat.

To date (2001), it has not yet been turned into a film but there are rumors that this could happen in the near future. The novel continues to be read for pleasure and studied by a wide range of international readers. In the UK it appears on A level syllabuses, and on university and adult continuing education syllabuses both sides of the Atlantic, and throughout the world. *Alias Grace* has made a considerable contribution to Margaret Atwood's reputation as a novelist, as did the earlier *The Handmaid's Tale*, and her *Blind Assassin* (2000 — which won the Booker Prize).

*Alias Grace* helped Atwood win several prizes and awards including the Premio Mondello (1997), Salon Magazine Best Fiction of 1997, Best Local Author, NOW Magazine Readers' Poll (1996 and 1997), Norwegian Order of Literary Merit (1996), The Giller Prize (1996), and Canadian Booksellers Association Author of the Year (1996).

## ATWOOD ON THE WEB

Margaret Atwood has a considerable presence on the internet with a variety of websites developed by fans, and one which she manages herself. Atwood's presence on the internet, on her own site, in readings and book signings, testifies to her interest in staying in touch with her reading public.

On February 11, 1997, (the year after *Alias Grace* was published) the Margaret Atwood Society's Atwood Discussion List (Atwood-L) was launched. This e-conferencing list, hosted by the University College of the Cariboo, is open to anyone with an interest in researching, teaching, studying, or reading Atwood's works. The list serves as a medium for discussion and a place to post questions and comments. Members of the Atwood Society are automatically subscribed to Atwood-L as a feature of membership.

Atwood herself has made several documents, essays, and lectures related to *Alias Grace* available online for those who wish to pursue further the scholarship around the facts of the real case and some of the motivation behind the book. In her lecture "Spotty-Handed Villainesses" (1994) Atwood uses Rebecca West, Huxley, James, Stoker, Austen, and Shakespeare and her own mail to back up her argument, a spur to her creation of the fictionalized Grace, that since "women have more to them than virtue," some of the evil in women needs putting back into our stories. Innovative literature tends to include the excluded, she argues, and introducing conflict and action, changing stereotypical views, are all part of the novelist's quest to entertain and provoke response. In the later "Ophelia has a Lot to answer For" (1997) she focuses on recreating/reinventing Grace Marks in the Toronto Lunatic asylum in her mission to explore ways in which society constructs and represents women as hysterical, mad, nervous, and the contemporary scientific and pseudo-scientific explanations for such constructions of madness. The debates about Grace's real or faked madness linked to and were contextualized in contemporary perceptions and representations of women, both in the nineteenth century and for us reading Atwood's tale. Also internet published and part of her source material is a letter from G. Duggan Jnr (August 11, 1843), part of Jack C. Arnell's collection of transatlantic postal history. Duggan was a friend of Thomas Kinnear's and the letter, with newspaper cutting enclosed, tells his relatives of his shocking deception and death. Grace Marks' own responses (1848–1864) to the questionnaire on her liberation from the Pententiary are also available on Atwood's O. W. Toad (a play on the word Atwood) website. Grace, a prisoner for 28 years and ten months, was generally satisfied with the conditions of her stay, but found it difficult to recognize any guilt herself. When Grace was asked (p. 23):

"What has been the general cause of your misfortunes and what has been the immediate cause of the crime for which you have been sent to the Penitentiary?"

She answered.

"Having been employed in the same house with a villain." (Marks, 1872)

## MARGARET ATWOOD SOCIETY

There is a Margaret Atwood society. Aimed at longer term readers and fans of Atwood, it can be joined by contacting the treasurer, Professor Mary Kirtz of the University of Akron, at:

Department of English
University of Akron
Akron, Ohio 44325
U.S.A.

It publishes a semi-annual newsletter with articles on Atwood, information about her public appearances and speeches, and news about her forthcoming books. Additionally, the society publishes an annual bibliography of Atwood's publications and reviews of her work. For more details about submission requirements, contact Professor Rosenberg.

Jerome Rosenberg
English Department
Miami University
Oxford, Ohio 45056
U.S.A.

*http://www.cariboo.bc.ca/atwood/atwoodsociety.htm*

There is a Margaret Atwood information site which Atwood manages and contributes to herself at:

*http://www.web.net/owtoad/welcome.html/*

This site contains information on "Life & Times," on writing, books by and about Margaret Atwood, frequently asked questions, links to several interviews and essays, and notes from Atwood herself.

She writes about writing and getting published in "The Rocky Road to Paper Heaven," which includes information on overcoming a variety of pitfalls including writer's block, poor agents, working well with an editor and *not* just treating them as the "room service" of publishing.

Atwood's *Negotiating with the Dead* (2002) is her most in-depth treatment of what it means to be a writer, and her views on the interactions between writers, materials, texts and readers. Constructed from a series of lectures Atwood delivered at Cambridge University in 2001, the book illustrates her remarkably wide reading: from Chaucer to Ian McEwan; from fairytales and myths to established and contemporary classics, as well as popular fiction writers like Elmore Leonard and Patricia Cornwell. Recognising the importance of the legacy of other tales and other writers, Atwood uses Gothic strategies and references: vampirism, trips to the underworld, the spinning and unraveling of stories. 'The dead get blood . . . they are assumed to be hungry and thirsty. In return, the poet gets clairvoyance, and the completion of her identify as a poet. It's an old argument. All writers learn from the dead.' (p. 178)

Atwood is a very accessible author in the sense that she conducts readings internationally to introduce readers to her new novels. She comments on her own website, but she also maintains strict personal and public regimes and access to her through interviews is handled by supportive administrative staff.

# 5

# Further Reading and Discussion Questions

## DISCUSSION QUESTIONS

There are several questions which can inform our reading and discussion of Margaret Atwood and her contemporaries, most of which have been explored in our discussions of *Alias Grace*. Two key areas of questions (which can be asked in several different ways) are:

1. How does Atwood critique representations of women and constructions of gender in *Alias Grace*?
2. How does she explore and critique the various traditional and cultural myths which constrain and construct men and women?

Grace herself is both a victim and manipulator of late nineteenth century versions of women as innocent victims or hysterical demons. As potential murderess, she is on the receiving end of others' fascination with and doubts about women's evil. "Was Grace a female fiend and temptress?" asks Atwood. Grace tells of visits from "jelly-like" ladies (p. 73), and discussion of the "Woman Question," aware how society constructs and represents her and others. If she is a love-crime dupe, she can be pitied, it is a romantic tale. Alternatively, she could change our views about women's potential for violent crimes. Under psychoanalysis from Simon Jordan, Grace both becomes confused with his secret childhood based fantasies about the sexual attractiveness of homely women (pp. 139, 382), (Grace sewing reminds him of the maids with whom he flirted; Grace resembles a fatally alluring mermaid) and herself, and seizes his weaknesses to stitch him a tale of her gradually recalled innocence.

Simon Jordan is vulnerable to women's attractions and wiles, and his version of women, onto whom he offloads his problems and needs. He is disastrously taken in by both Grace and his bony landlady. McDermott, Grace's partner in crime, is seen straightforwardly as guilty and hanged. Society finds it easier to punish men for violent crimes.

3. How do we know what is historical fact and what fiction in *Alias Grace*? How does Margaret Atwood interrogate and problematize versions and representations of fact and history, showing them to be constructions themselves affected by point of view, context, intentions, author, and audience?

"I will embroider" (p. 459) says Grace. It is impossible to track down the absolute facts of any event in history and Atwood's text makes this plain by bringing together newspaper reports, ballads, first person records, psychoanalytically based recollections, and numerous contemporary factual and fictional responses to and reports of the Grace Marks case. You could look at the variety of versions of history, for example the newspaper: "McDermott . . . was morose and churlish . . . Grace was of a lively disposition" (p. 183). Consider how Grace tells us she constructs tales for Simon Jordan, who seeks the truth (bringing her root vegetables to jolt a memory of cellars and hidden murders). Even records of Grace's testimony recognize her embroidering of the truth "She is an accomplished and a most practised liar" (p. 71). At the novel's end, we still do not know the full details of the murder, which leads us to deduce that it is impossible to reach any truth not affected by point of view, intention, context.

4. In what ways and to what ends does Atwood use the central metaphor of quilting in the novel?

Quilting is largely a woman's art and Grace Marks' story is a crafted product from her own memory and imagination, stitched together for both the psychoanalyst Simon Jordan, and the readers. Quilting suggests sisterhood and creativity, and this is a women's story, a woman who has possibly been misrepresented because of the divisive "virgin or whore/angel or demon" versions of women at that time. Quilting also suggests the pulling together of a variety of versions of events — newspapers, scrapbooks, ballads, personal testimony — to try and form an overall interpreted pattern. This is the shape and part of the message of the novel. It is a compilation of different versions of events, memories and fictions, and it comments on the constructed, partial versions we have of anyone's story and of historical events. Quilting images and patterns are also referenced as themes and structural elements of different chapters.

5. How does her work provide interpretations and reinterpretations of specifically Canadian cultural myths and representations?

Other areas of questioning which are of interest could cover issues such as:

6. In what ways can her work be said to be "Canadian Gothic?"
7. How did she fit in with and relate to or influence other Canadian women writers? Are their concerns similar?
8. How does she fit in with and relate to or influence other contemporary women writers? Are their concerns similar?

When reading Margaret Atwood's work we can usefully consider how she fits in with the writing of other Canadian women writers, some First Nations or indigenous writers, some of immigrant descent. Like Atwood, many other contemporary Canadian women writers question cultural myths and constraints, critique romantic fictions and investigate what seem to be fixed versions, fixed interpretations of what it means to be a woman in contemporary, or historical Canada.

**FURTHER READING**

### Other Canadian Women Writers

*Alice Munro*

Alice Munro's short stories (1997) concentrate on rural and small town lives, obsessions and frustrated passions. Munro depicts lives of hope and constraint in wry, carefully wrought vignettes. Many of her women are alone, constrained by small communities, lack of love and hope, lack of any kind of positive future. They suffer restricted minds and places. Some are victims of the isolation and deprivation of rural communities. They lose children, their opportunities to work are curtailed, trapped in small homes as family servants, spinsters, widows, and daughters working for parents. Gossip dominates their lives as does a dated, imported colonialism emerging as stuffy coffee mornings and tea parties, curtailed opportunities. There is a great deal of poverty and family-based violence in these small town homes. Munro's wry, ironic short stories capture details of feelings, clothing, and mannerisms. One woman loses the chance for love, deceived by a lover who moves away and marries someone else. Another, a piano teacher ("Dance of the Happy Shades") produces an embarrassing yearly show for the mothers, their offspring repeating the same tunes as the mothers once played. Poignant moments and cruel vignettes identify each of Munro's characters as individuals: small people in small towns.

### Margaret Laurence

Small town constraints, and family tensions also dominate Margaret Laurence's *A Bird in the House* ([1970] 1994) a semi-fictionalized autobiography. Vanessa, the lonely child and growing author, listens into the lives and debates of her elders. Bible and pioneer myths inform her thought processes and early writing. When she discovers her tyrannical grandfather was himself a pioneer, she abandons her first written story, a pioneer tale, "Pillars of the Nation," written in her scribbler. An autocrat, he does irreparable damage to the lives of the women and men around him, thwarting and dominating them.

Women's lives are harsh, or dull and constrained. Edna, the unmarried aunt, cannot find work as a stenographer and lives at home, doing housemaid's work, her possibilities of finding a partner dwindling as each male visitor is subjected to the grandfather's scrutiny and verbal attack. Bigot and bully, the grandfather dominates everyone's hearing, rocking his chair angrily in the cellar. His cruel outbursts prevent relationships developing, minds flourishing. Even Vanessa's gentle imaginative cousin, Cliff, is harmed by the grandfather's meanness.

Insights into family passions and thoughts are delicately wrought and compelling reading. This is a tale of the restricted lives of middle class colonial and post-colonial women who cannot escape the constraints of their families, class, culture, or location. It is also a tale of a growing author, and as such, to some extent, it is a fallible narration which reveals its own narrative strategies in terms of what Vanessa misunderstands, ignores or focuses on with her limited child's perspective.

### Carol Shields

Carol Shields also explores pioneering and restricted lives. *Mary Swann* (1987) links women's artistic production, or restraints on it, and the isolation and sufferings of a poor, pioneering life. It seems that through the aid of her librarian friend, the poetry of a working class, relatively uneducated, rural woman, is published and discovered by the literary intelligentsia of California and New York. The worlds of poverty and deprivation of Mary Swann and the appropriating activities of the literati are contrasted, as are versions of fictionalizing raging from promotion, semi-fictionalized autobiography to biography. A New York woman publisher, becoming more closely embroiled in local lives, eventually decides not to write Swann's biography but to leave her in peace. The novel provides an interesting comparison with Atwood's *Alias Grace* when the real writer and her real life are discovered, contrasting with expectations and versions constructed around her literary reputation.

Shields' *The Stone Diaries* (1993 — Booker prize) concentrates on the lives of a harsh Scottish settler and his daughter. Along with the Irish (in *Alias Grace*), the Scottish settled in large numbers in

Canada and a common activity for Celtic and non-Celtic settlers has latterly become that of tracing family trees. This novel uses recollection, reconstruction of historical fact, and revisiting various memories and fictions of the family, in ways like *Alias Grace*. The novel opens with the daughter's birth and her mother's death, circling back to recount her parents' courtship, and her reticent father's great sorrow at his wife's death marked by the construction of a huge stone edifice. A local marvel, this artwork, the only emotional outpouring this stony-man can manage, does not last and is ultimately rather pointless.

### Aritha Van Herk

Aritha van Herk reclaims women's mythical power and active sexuality. Like Atwood, she dispels the illusions of traditional romance, undercutting representations of passive virginal women, asserting:

I come from the west, kingdom of the male virgin. . . . To be female and not-virgin, making stories in the kingdom of the male virgin, is dangerous. . . . Try being a writer there. Try being a woman there. (van Herk, 1984, p. 15)

In *No Fixed Address* (1989 [1986]) her protagonist, Arachne, subverts traditional constructions of women as marriage seekers, taking sexual pleasure where she finds it. Like the protagonist in Atwood's *Surfacing*, Arachne moves into the wilderness suggesting alternative women's freedoms. Finding the rock shape of a Wild Woman high up, she lies down in its form, expressing freedom. Like *Alias Grace*, this novel echoes a specifically woman's form: Arachne is a sales representative in ladies underwear and a series of different colored panties trail her across Canada, labeling chapters.

Van Herk also rewrites myths including, in *Judith* (1978), the

Persephone/Pluto myth as Judith attempts to find her new identity and avoid a cosmeticized self, re-establishing contact with a childhood self.

### First Nations Writers

Indigenous or First Nations people are largely absent from Atwood's work, but several First Nations writers deal, as does Atwood, with issues of identity, the limitations and erasure of history and memory, and the often duplicitous expression through writing. As with other indigenous writers such as Australian Aboriginal writers Sally Morgan and Ruby Langford, Maria Campbell and others use the semi-fictionalized autobiographical form enabling personal, historical, and imaginative evocation of experiences, much as Grace's first person recall and narrative does in Atwood's novel. Lenore Keshing-Tobias, Lee Maracle, Ruby Slipperjack, and Beatrice Culleton are notable First Nations writers.

### Maria Campbell

Campbell's semi-fictionalized autobiographical *Halfbreed* (1974) was the first novel published by a Canadian First Nations or indigenous Indian writer. It was followed by the play which it inspired, *The Book of Jessica: A Theatrical Transformation* (1986) with Linda Griffiths. Campbell experienced the separation of living in native communities and the stigma of being of mixed race or "M'tis" (a negative term, mestizzo, of mixed race, more recently replaced by "biracial," or "hybrid"). She learned self-reliance and self-worth from her pipe-smoking grandmother Cheechum, and at the novel's end, expresses self-discovery and community identity: "I have brothers and sisters all over the country, I no longer need my blanket to survive" (Campbell, 1974, in Vizenor, 1995, p. 75). Campbell's reclamation of the term "half-breed" is a powerful linguistic move.

The novel contains recurrent, positive images of love, nature, beauty, and peace mitigating against the harshness of the protagonist's life.

### Jeannette Armstrong

Jeannette Armstrong, children's writer and novelist, is director of the En'Owkin School of International writing in the Okanagan, British Columbia. Children's novels include *Enwhisteetkwa: Walk on Water* (1982) and *Neekna and Chemia* (1984). Her adult work *Slash* (1985) concerns a young man involved in the struggle for aboriginal rights. In "This is a Story" (in Thieme 1996, pp. 428–433) she tells a tale within a tale, a Trickster tale of Kyoti, an Okanagan man who returns to his home area when things have deteriorated and the salmon runs are blocked up by the invaders. Kyoti uses natural magical powers to restore the salmon runs. In oral storytelling modes, straightforward factual phrases, dialogue, and yet often fantasy situations, Armstrong evokes the magical moment, asserting its authenticity as a way of reading the situation:

That story happened. I tell you that much. It's a powerful one, I tell it now because it's true. (Armstrong in Thieme, 1996, p. 432)

Her work is engaged, utilizing Native Canadian Indian mythology and dealing with issues of equality and land rights.

### Other Writers

Writing by experimental women writers, by immigrant, lesbian, and indigenous writers, has flourished since the latter part of the 1980s. Lola Lemire Tostevin's poetry concentrates on women's bodily and linguistic construction in *Color of her Speech* (1982), *Gynotext*

(1983), and *Double Standards* (1985). Daphne Marlatt writes a free verse/journal in *Touch to My Tongue* (1984) and a poetic novel, *Ana Historica* (1988). Jane Rule writes of representations of women's sexuality. Kristjana Gunnar's lyrical novel *The Prowler* (1989) considers ways in which exploitative imperialism affects her family through successive generations. Marlene Nourbese Philip looks at the overwhelming impression of the English language. Dionne Brand in *Primitive Offensive* (1982), *No Language is Neutral* (1990), short stories *Sans Souci* (1988) and criticism, investigates racism, colonialism, lesbianism, and her own identity. Poetry and fiction by Asian Canadians such as Joy Kogawa (*Obasan* 1993) is also growing.

### Non-Canadian Contemporary Women Writers

Margaret Atwood is a leading contemporary woman writer, and we might also like to ask in what ways she relates to, compares, or contrasts with other women writers from the UK, the United States, and elsewhere. Along with Atwood, writers such as Fay Weldon and Angela Carter, Michele Roberts, Emma Tennant, and Joyce Carol Oates, critique representations of women and the myths which constrain and construct men and women in contemporary society. They use magic, the supernatural, and history, linking real or realistic events with the imaginative life, the life of the imagination and the spirit, providing information about people's feelings about their lives. Their work also uses intertextual references, placing it in the context of earlier writing dealing in similar or different ways with issues of identity, relationships, gender, women's lives, and roles, the ways in which we construct and represent life and values through various fictionalizing and documentary processes. Gothic is a common feature of these writers.

How does Atwood use the Gothic in her work? And how does

this relate to other contemporary women Gothic writers? Margaret Atwood's work can be said to be "Canadian Gothic" in that it utilizes the Gothic, frequently a form used to critique social constructions, and does so located in, exploring and exposing, the concerns of Canadian people and the Canadian context. As Gothic writing, it uses characteristics of the Gothic such as opposites, paradoxes, and twinning. Exposing the dark side of conformity, alternatives to the status quo, it is contradictory, providing social critique and highlighting what lies beneath everyday behaviors, what hidden contradictions, dreams, fantasies, and fears undermine the ostensibly familiar and ordinary.

### Angela Carter

Like Atwood, Angela Carter is a Gothic writer who critiques representations of women's roles. Carter demythologises myths which construct and constrain women's lives. In her early work she rewrites conventional fairytales such as those of the Brothers Grimm and Perrault, exposing their latent sexism. In rewriting the Bluebeard myth (also a favorite of Atwood's) in "The Bloody Chamber" (1967), Carter exposes the dangerous sado-masochistic mutual attraction of the young impoverished girl for the older, wealthy Duke who offers her a paternalistic seeming relationship, a front for tyranny. On his temporary departure he hands her the house keys, giving her free run of the castle but forbidding one specific room. Of course she opens it. Inside she finds the bodies of his previous wives, a fate which she then realizes awaits her because of her challenge to his power, her seeking after knowledge. In the traditional tale, she is rescued by her brothers. In Carter's version, her warrior mother comes to the rescue. The girl settles down with a blind piano tuner, her support during her ordeal.

Carter's rewriting exposes the latent sado-masochism in such stories, undercutting the patriarchal conventions which would on the one hand indicate to women that challenging male power by seeking knowledge (opening the room) is dangerous, and on the other that the only form of rescue in their disempowered condition, is by other males. Carter's young woman in this story as in "The Company of Wolves," a feminist version of the fairytale "Little Red Riding Hood," recognizes her own sexuality and its dangers, seizing power and identity. Later stories by Angela Carter critique the "Living Doll" infantalizing and disempowering image of women, and myths which render women both seductive and fatal, clearly to be punished for their sexuality and threat. This threat, Carter suggests, is one produced by male fears of women's individualism and sexuality. In *The Magic Toyshop*, the tale of orphaned Melanie critiques sexual power games. In so doing it exposes ways in which a variety of myths and texts operate to condition the expectations and constraints on girls and women.

### Fay Weldon

Another writer critiquing constrained roles for and representations of women using myth, magic, and humor, is Fay Weldon. Weldon's *The Life and Loves of a She Devil* focuses on one woman's rebellion against the constraints of domesticity and the lies of romantic fictions which affect women's sense of their own purpose and their own narratives. Ruth a "monstrous" woman living in a suburban housing state, on Eden Grove, is unable to conform to domestic expectations. When her accountant husband Bobbo has an affair with Mary Fisher, romantic fiction novelist (whose novels are partly to blame for unrealistic romantic fantasies read and internalized by women), Ruth leaves all the domestic appliances on full, the house catches alight (as it could so easily do) and leaves Bobbo to look after the children.

The novel exposes the unreality of romantic fiction with great comic effects. Fay Weldon might be giving women the last laugh. Reunited with Bobbo, Ruth, who has remodeled herself, is now in control.

Weldon's novels use magic and humor to critique the constrained lives of women and the cultural myths which ensure this constraint. In *Growing Rich*, three Fenland girls, doomed to dead end jobs, are tempted by the Devil's henchman, Driver, who cruises past in his Black BMW offering one girl, Carmen, everything she might desire, if she will be the consort of Sir Bernard Bellamy, local magnate, whose soul Driver seeks to own. Carmen refuses, but her refusals bring job losses, spots, and bad luck to her and those around her. Carmen manages to fool this Mephisotophelean figure, eventually marrying Sir Bernard, and also saving his soul, largely through the token of her own virginity — ever a magic talisman for women. Fay Weldon's work, like Atwood's, demythologizes the myths which constrain women's representations.

## Pat Barker

Other writers reinterpreting historical moments and events include Pat Barker, whose work initially concentrated on lives of working-class women in the North of England, Preston. *Union Street*, a series of short stories building into a novel, considers women in a single street, their ages ranging from a young girl to an old woman, their lives encompassing a series of hardships, abusive or absent partners, rape, abortion, prostitution, penury, and some sisterhood and support. Harsh lives of similar women are also explored in *Blow the House Down* and *The Century's Daughter*.

With her trilogy *Regeneration, The Eye in the Door,* and *The Ghost Road* however, Barker moved into new territory of New Historicism, making readers aware of the constructedness and gendered nature of history. Unusually for a woman writer, Pat Barker takes World War I as her subject, focusing on the lives of poets Siegfried Sassoon and Wilfred Owen, and Rivers, the doctor who treated Owen for shell shock at Craiglockheart. Barker's narratives concentrate on the more female side of life and consciousness, on poetic expression, the domestic, caring, and awareness of the absurdity of war. Barker also considers how the daily experience of war encourages a maternal instinct in young men stuck in the trenches, and how women gained recognition for their work abilities, some independence in the enforced absence of their often abusive husbands.

We can see, as we do in *Alias Grace*, that the imposition of particular versions of reality and truth are culturally constructed: with all the emphasis of ethnicity, class, and gender which this implies.

# Bibliography

### Selected Works by Atwood

Atwood, Margaret. "Progressive Insanities of a Pioneer" in John Thieme, ed. *The Arnold Anthology of Post-Colonial Literature in English.* London: Edward Arnold 1996.

Atwood, Margaret. *Survival: a Thematic Guide to Canadian literature* Toronto: Asanti (1996) [1972].

Atwood, Margaret. *The Journals of Susannah Moodie.* London: Virago. 1970.

Atwood, Margaret. *Surfacing.* London: Virago. 1972.

Atwood, Margaret. *The Edible Woman.* London: Virago. 1969.

Atwood, Margaret. *Lady Oracle.* London: Virago. 1976.

Atwood, Margaret. *Bodily Harm.* London: Virago. 1981.

Atwood, Margaret. *The Handmaid's Tale.* London: Virago. 1985.

Atwood, Margaret. *The Robber Bride.* London: Bloomsbury. 1993.

Atwood, Margaret. *Alias Grace,* London: QPD. 1996.

Atwood, Margaret. *The Blind Assassin.* London:Bloomsbury. 2000.

Atwood, Margaret. *Negotiating with the Dead: A Writer on Writing.* Cambridge: CUP. 2002.

Atwood, M. "Reader's Companion to *Alias Grace* by Margaret Atwood. A letter from Margaret Atwood." 1996.

[online]: *www.readinggroupguides.com/guides.alias-graceauthor.html*

Atwood, M. "Ophelia has a lot to answer for" (Lecture) 1997
    [online]: *http://www.web.net/owtoad/ophelia.html* January 4, 2002.
Atwood, M. "Spotty-handed Villainesses" (Lecture) 1994.
    [online]: *http://www.web.net/owtoad/vlness.html* (January 4, 2002.


### Reviews of *Alias Grace*

Arias, R. "How Can I Be All of These Different Things at Once? Fiction
    and History in *Alias Grace* by Margaret Atwood." 2000.
    [online]:    *http://www.eng.helsinki.fi/doe/ESSE5-2000/rosario.arias.htm*
    March 23, 2001.
Basbanes, N. A. "Margaret Atwood: Lizzie Borden's Tale." 1997.
    [online]: *http://womenswriters.about.com/library/blatwood.htm*  Dec  5,
    2001.
Duguid, L. "Books: If truth be told." *The Guardian*, p. 14 October 3, 1996.
Freely, M. "Books: What is Grace's guilty secret? And will she ever come
    out from under that quilt?" *The Observer*, p. 18 Sept 22, 1996.
Kemp, P. "A Gorgeous patchwork of art." Fiction. *Sunday Times*, p. 11.
    Sept 8, 1996.
LeClair, T. "Quilty Verdict." (1996)
    [online]: *http://www.past.thenation.com/issue/961209/1209lect.htm*. De-
    cember 5, 2001.
Lehmann-Haupt, C. "Did She Or Didn't She? A Tale of Two Murders."
    (1996).
    [online]:    *www.belgonet.be/bn000309Margaret%20Atwood%2020Alias%*
    *20Grace.htm*. March 28, 2001.
Mantel, H. "Murder & Memory." 1996
    [online]: *http://nybooks.com/articles/article-preview?article_id=1316* De-
    cember 5, 2001.
Moore, A. "Margaret Atwood's Latest Novel Pieces Together a Compelling
    Collision Between Science And Mysticism." (1997)
    [online]:    *www.weeklywire.com/tw/01-16-97/review3.htm*.   December  5,
    2001.
Pepinster, C. "The Writer's Tale: How a story chose an author and wowed

the critics; Canada's top author tells Catherine Pepinster about her new book's spiritual inspiration." *The Independent*, p. 9. Sept 20, 1996.

Prose, F. "Death and the Maid." *New York Times* (Late Edition-Final). December 29, 1996.

Rogerson, M. "Reading the Patchworks in *Alias Grace*." *Journal of Commonwealth Literature* vol 33.1. Sydney, Australia : University of Sydney, p. 14. 1998.

Wiley, D. "Atwood At A Glance." Interview. 1996.
[online]: *http://womenwriters.about.com/library/blatwood.htm* April 14, 2001.


### Criticism of Atwood

Angier, C. "In the prison of male fantasy; Margaret Atwood's new novel is a Gothic tale of sex and class. *Alias Grace* by Margaret Atwood." *The Independent*, p. 5. Sept 14, 1996.

Davey, F. *Margaret Atwood: A Feminist Poetics*. Vancouver: Talonbooks. 1984.

Davidson, A. E., and C. N. (Eds.). *The Art of Margaret Atwood: Essays in Criticism*. Toronto: Anansi. 1981.

Stein, N, *Margaret Atwood*. Twayne Modern Author series. 2001.


### Other writers, other criticism

Brydon, Diana & Tiffin, Helen. *Decolonising Fictions*. Sydney: Dangaroo Press. 1993.

Brydon, Diana. "Landscape and authenticity." *Dalhousie Review*, 61, 2 (Summer). 1981.

Kroetsch, Robert. (1974) "Unhiding the Hidden", *Journal of Canadian Fiction* 3, 3, p. 43.

New, W. H. A *History of Canadian Literature*. London: Macmillan. 1989.

Palmateer Pennee, Donna. "Canadian women's literary discourse in English 1982–92." In Anna Rutherford, Lars Jensen, and Shirley Chew (eds.), *Not the Nineties: post-colonial women's writing*. New South Wales: Dangaroo Press. 1994.

Van Herk, Aritha. "Women writers and the prairie: spies in an indifferent landscape." *Kunapipi*, 6,2 p. 15. 1984.

Vizenor, Gerald. (ed.). *Native American Literature*. New York: Harpercollins. 1995.


## Works by other writers

Barker, Pat. *Union Street*. London: Virago
———— *Regeneration*. Harmondsworth : Penguin.
———— *The Eye in the Door*. Harmondsworth : Penguin.
———— *The Ghost Road*. Harmondsworth : Penguin.
Brand, Dionne. *Primitive Offensive*. Canada, Williams Wallace. 1982.
———— *Sans Souci*. Canada, Williams Wallace. 1988.
———— *No Language is Neutral*. Toronto: Coach House. 1990.
Campbell, Maria. "The Little People" in (ed.) Vizenor, *Native American Literature*. New York: Harpercollins, extract from (1973) *Halfbreed*. University of Nebraska Press and McClelland and Stewart: Toronto. 1995.
Carter, Angela. "The Company of Wolves." *The Bloody Chamber*, London: Virago 1967.
Carter, Angela. *The Magic Toyshop*. London: Virago 1967.
Duggan, G. "A Letter to J. Skelton Esq., Peterhead, Scotland from G. Duggan Jr, Toronto, Canada." In Richmond Hil Public Library. 1843. [online]: http://www.web.net/owtoad/kinnear2.html
Gunnar, Kristjana. *The Prowler*. Red Deer College. 1989.
Kogawa, Joy. *Obasan*. Harmondsworth: Penguin. 1981.
Laurence, Margaret. *A Bird in the House*. Toronto: Mclelland and Stewart. 1994 [1970].
Lemire Tostevin, Lola. *Color of her Speech*. Toronto : Coach House. 1982.
Lemire Tostevin, Lola. *Gynotext*. Toronto: Underwhich. 1983.
Lemire Tostevin, Lola. *Double Standards*. Toronto: Longspoon. 1985.
Marks, G. "Answers to Liberation Questionnaire." Kingston Penitentiary, 6 August 1872, from *The Inspector's Minute Book*. February 3, 1848–October 1, 1864, p. 480. Correctional services Museum of Canada, Kingston Ontario. 1872.
[online]: http://www.web.net/owtoad/liberati.html (January 4, 2002.

Marlatt, Daphne. *Touch to My Tongue*. Toronto: Longspoon. 1984.

Marlatt, Daphne. *Ana Historica*. Toronto : Coach House. 1988.

Moodie, Susannah. *Roughing it in the Bush or Life in Canada*. Carl Ballstadt, ed. Ottawa: Carleton University Press. 1988[1852].

Munro, Alice. *Selected Stories*. London: Vintage. 1997.

Niatum, Duane, (ed). *Harper's Anthology of 20th Century Native American Poetry*. San Francisco: Harpercollins. 1988.

Shields, Carol. *Mary Swann*. London : Fourth Estate 1987.

——— *The Stone Diaries*. London: Fourth Estate. 1993.

Shikatani, Gerry. "Here, not There" in (ed.) Juliana Chang, *Quiet Fires, a Historical Anthology of Asian American poetry 1892–1970*. New York: The Asian American Writers Workshop. 1996.

Van Herk, Aritha. *Judith*. London: Corgi. 1978.

——— *No Fixed Address*. London: Virago. 1989 [1986].

Weldon, Fay. *The Life and Loves of a She-Devil*. London: Flamingo, HarperCollins. 1983.

——— *Growing Rich*. London : Harpercollins. 1992.